IN THE WORDS OF
OLYMPIC PENINSULA AUTHORS

Volume 2

Thirty authors joined words to create this imaginative anthology. Together, we celebrate the Olympic Peninsula of Washington State, which inspires all of us.

We are a diverse lot, from age eleven to nobody's business, from world-wise to homegrown, from humorists to heartbreakers.

We delight in sharing our knowledge, opinions, imagination, and emotions with you. We hope you feel the spirit of the Olympic Peninsula as you read the stories, poems and essays that await you inside.

IN THE WORDS OF
OLYMPIC PENINSULA AUTHORS
Volume 2

Compiled and edited by Linda B. Myers and Heidi Hansen
Cover design and photo by Alan Halfhill
Interior design by Heidi Hansen

Published by H3 Press, Carlsborg, WA.

ISBN: 978-0998252650

Acknowledgement is made for permission to publish:

DEDICATION

In the Words of Olympic Peninsula Authors, Volume 2,
is dedicated to the people, past and present,
who have found strength
and inspiration in the spirit of the area.

CONTENTS

CONTENTS

IN THE WORDS OF
OLYMPIC PENINSULA AUTHORS
Volume 2

Author Intro

LILY TODD

As a child I loved stories. Mom told a lot of them. I spent much of my childhood in fantasy land. I could travel, be anything, and do anything. This offered so much freedom, I preferred it to playmates.

Eventually, I was forced to grow up. Responsibilities, marriage, children, and jobs do that. Of course, I navigated to bookkeeping; it was paper and pencils in those days. Then I discovered real estate, a wide world of properties and people, each with a story to tell.

My real estate career spans several decades. Last century, it encompassed the Rocky Mountains of Montana and the bustling (to me) city of Spokane. This century I took on the challenges of southern California and finally the tree-infused, mountain-crested and salt water-caressed Olympic Peninsula. Now I am home, living, working, and writing here.

For me, writing is just another way to have fun and be in complete control of my environment. I will write and read on.

Lily can be reached at authorlil@wavecable.com.

THE LIFE OF AN AGNEW FARMER'S WIFE

Doris rises with the sun, like she does three seasons of the year. Summers are the hardest as the sun comes up earlier and earlier. Winters are time for rest, unless it is below freezing. Then she stokes the fire every five hours to keep the home warm.

Her mother trained her well. Never dwell on the chores coming the day ahead or next week or next month. Just focus on the task at hand and relish each item as it comes. "The future, with a little help from us, will take care of itself," Ma always said.

So with joy in her heart, or as close to joy as she comes, Doris dresses, makes the bed and goes downstairs to start this day the Lord made. She says her usual prayers as she plugs in the coffee pot, *Your will be done,* followed by *may all our blessings be pleasant today.*

Like a queen surveying her kingdom, she checks the kitchen for anything out of place, scans the screened porch to make sure the raccoons stayed outside last night, and opens the screen door to view the garden and weather.

Looks like rain, she thinks, as she considers the darkening sky. Rain clouds push at the Olympic Mountains. *I have time to pick the peas before starting breakfast, if I fix the mister scrambled eggs and toast. Then, if it rains, I'll do the peas.*

Before the last thought ends, she grabs the battered pail and is in the garden stripping the bushes of any pod two-thirds or fuller. Frantically filling a second and third bucket, she finishes, barely in time. The rain is here, and it is not a gentle spring shower.

Rushing to the kitchen, she reminds herself to turn up the heat on the pan just a little for two minutes. Smiling she thanks Granny Jones for that trick. As she reaches for the fry pan, she pauses to give thanks to the long line of farmer's wives before her and the many shortcuts they discovered and passed on.

By lunch time, she puts twenty-seven pints of peas in the cellar. Two loads of folded laundry wait to be carried upstairs. Just as she removes the hamburger patty from the fry pan, the mister comes in the back door. It is straight up noon.

Taking his place at the head of the table, he nods his thanks at the platter set in front of him. Words are few and far between. The efficient routine developed over thirty-three years controls their lives. Each moves to the music of the seasons and the hours of the clock like a choreographed dance. If either wants a change, the other is unaware.

And so the hours, days, weeks, and years pass. Doris is content until the farm next door sells to a couple from California. As soon as the moving van leaves, Doris takes the newcomers an apple pie still warm from her oven.

For the occasion, she dresses in a clean frock only two years old. Looking at the dress, she notices it has faded a little but not enough for most people to observe.

As she raises her hand to knock, the door is yanked open, and a raspy voice demands to know what she is doing here. Stammering, Doris says, "I'm your neighbor to the west, and I brought a pie to welcome you to our community."

Stepping through the doorway is a brittle blond in a pair of designer blue jeans and a LA sweatshirt two sizes too big. Smoke from the cigarette dangling between her lips surrounds her head like a halo. "How nice," the newcomer grates as she smiles and extends her hand. Doris is still backing up. She stops and, stepping forward, places the pie in the outstretched palm.

"Where are my manners?" the new neighbor croaks. "I'm Marilou. Come on in."

The newcomer does not fit in with the local crowd. No one in the farming community calls her by name, just says that newcomer. Everyone knows who they are talking about. She is never without a cigarette in her mouth except when she is mashing one out and replacing it with a new stick. When forced to carry on a conversation, locals attempt to stand upwind and as far away from the smoke as possible.

Her husband seems a right nice guy. At the Agnew Feed Store on Old Olympic Highway, he asks for someone to help get his farm producing again. Ben, a neighbor's son who is a little slow, starts working with him. Ben says Mr. Brown learns fast and really cares about the ground and animals.

Now Doris's days include the latest information about the strange pair next door. No rumor is too small or too strange to be followed and believed. Mr. Brown is the opposite of his wife, charming and courteous. People like him and soon begin calling him by his first name, William.

The seasons pass. William takes to farming like he was born to it. His fields are the greenest in the area. His cattle bring the highest prices at auction in the fall.

Soon two years lapse from the time the moving van arrived. William comes by a few times a week to buy eggs. His wife does not like chickens. Soon he is staying for a cup of coffee. The mister just snorts and says daylight's for working, not visiting.

Doris fails to notice that her house is even cleaner than it was before or that she is using hand lotion more. She does not see the spring in her step or observe that on egg day, as she calls it, the cookies or cakes are just a little special.

If the mister detects any change, he does not say.

Then the newcomer dies. The news ripples through the area and questions are asked: Will William stay? Will he go?

Doris takes the required casserole to the newcomer's home soon after she hears the news. A whole parcel of strange people fills the driveway, yard, and house. Some gussied up woman takes the dish with a thank you and closes the door before Doris can ask about William.

Doris wonders how, if at all, her life will change. Slowly she begins to realize how much egg day means to her. When the thought of William never coming again crosses her mind, feelings she never knew she has come calling. She closes her eyes and starts praying for pure thoughts and to be the wife she promised. Strangely, prayers do not help.

The wisdom she relies on does not come. Instead she sees pictures in her mind. William's house is freshly painted on the outside. His fences are mended. Flowers bloom around the home in a riot of colors. Lavender plants line the driveway. Doris's house needed painting when she and the mister moved in thirty-five years ago; it still does. Her only flowers are two spindly rose bushes, one white and one red, struggling to live by the back door.

She is alone with her pain and her shame for her meager existence. Even praying to the Lord does nothing to relieve her humiliation. Doris prays a little harder to be a good wife.

On the next egg day, William arrives looking worn and thinner. Apologizing for bothering her, he asks if she can triple his order, "All the guests, you know. And I'll need more for the next couple of weeks." She smiles and fills his order, knowing she has to go to Port Townsend to get the eggs he requested. Although that town requires a two-hour drive, she cannot be seen buying eggs in Sequim or Port Angeles. Her heart sings, he came, he came.

After he leaves she drops to her knees in the garden. She prays in a whisper, "Oh, Lord, take these feelings out of me. Turn me back into the wife I was just a few years ago. Make me appreciate the serenity I had, the joy in doing just my work."

Looking up into the cloudless blue sky, she calls on her guides, the farmers' wives who blazed the way before her. Doris begs to be shown the way back, back to the lackluster existence she always knew, back to safety, to non-feeling, to acceptance.

Instead, other wisdom passed down from one farmer's wife to another comes to her. To survive, a farmer's wife has to be tough, resilient. Finding ways to handle the best and worst Mother Nature provides is only one of the challenges.

Farming is dangerous. Men get hurt, sick or die. It is nigh to impossible for a woman to keep the land fertile and productive alone. A widow with a good farm and reputation for cooking, baking and caring is highly desirable.

However, a woman saddled with the wrong husband is just asking from trouble. Some men have a golden touch, turning profits from the soil no matter what the weather does. Other farmers may work as hard but are barely able to pay the bills. The Clallam County Tax Collector may be just one poor crop away from taking the valuable land. The women of the past whisper to her: "We are the true stewards of the ground. It is up to us to protect the farm, to keep it safe for future cultivators. There are ways to handle this problem."

After all, they tell her like planning next year's garden, keeping an eye for replacement stock is part of this process.

Meanwhile, the mister is having a run of bad luck. He is thirsty all the time. He asks if the food is saltier than normal. Shaking her head, Doris inquires if he needs to see old Doc. Halliday. Of course, the answer is no.

One day the big rear tractor tire comes off, rolling him and the machine down the hill. If it had fallen off a bit later where the land was steeper, he might have been killed.

Then their prize boar crashes through his pen at feeding time and almost knocks the farmer over. It's mating season, and pigs are unruly at this time.

As he is raising the hay lift to put a load in the loft, the rope breaks letting the lift and hay fall back down on him. A broken arm and badly turned knee send him to the house.

His pain killers do not work. Although he doubles and triples the dose, the pain from his swollen knee keeps him awake all night. The doctor changes the prescription and then changes it again. Finally, in exasperation, Old Doc Halliday tells him to man up. Soon he is wandering around in a daze. The only thing that helps the constant agony is the moonshine he buys behind the feed store.

The neighbors pitch in to do the outside work even though it is harvest time and everyone is busy. Many of them are just repaying the man for the help he willingly gave them over the years. The women come and sit with him so Doris can rest. They look at the mister with sad eyes.

Six weeks after the funeral, William comes by to help, too. He says it is good to have something else to think about and to be able to lend a hand to someone in need. He even sends his helper to do the morning and evening chores.

William still comes three times a week for eggs, although he uses fewer of them now. Strangely none of the other women are around at these times.

The mister is losing weight. He pushes food away saying it does not taste good. Unable to sleep, he roams the main floor of the house at night in his wheelchair. A body in pain cannot heal. Humans also need fuel to mend.

Finally, after five long weeks of no progress, Doris insists the mister comes back to their upstairs bedroom. With help, he climbs the steps and finally sinks into his comfortable old bed. Almost instantly he falls asleep.

A sudden sharp pain in his knee bolts him awake. He springs from the bed screaming. The pain is so intense, his only thought is to get his bottle of moonshine and quickly. He left the bottle in the living room. Staggering, he stumbles to the stairs only to trip over something. His last scream brings Doris from the bathroom. By the time she reaches the mister at the bottom of the stairs, he is dead.

The next spring, Doris rises with the sunrise, as usual. She quickly dresses, makes the bed which is a little more messed than normal and hurries downstairs. Humming to herself, she checks her domain, the kitchen, porch and garden. It is going to be another beautiful spring day.

Returning to the kitchen, she begins breakfast. Pancakes or waffles, she wonders as she places thick slices of bacon in the pan. Every meal is her favorite now. She and William linger over the food, sharing bits of news, tidbits from their pasts and plans for the future. *What a lucky day it was for me when he moved here.*

Author Intro

JOHN VICTOR ANDERSON

All the poems in this selection of my work were inspired by the rain and bloom of the Olympic Peninsula. I received my MFA in poetry from McNeese State University in 2007 and am currently ABD within the University of Louisiana at Lafayette English PhD program. I currently teach English for Peninsula College and Clallam Bay Corrections Center.

John can be reached at Johnvictoranderson@gmail.com

MERMAID TEARS

or call it *Sea Glass* if that cuts less,

breaks polished over, sun-stumbled

glints of tumbled time rumbled out

smoothed, wine rubble

condensed to frosted dew, jewels

forged inside this unseen wasteland

heart where even butterflies compete

lapping up the eyes of turtles

for tears salted, hard won, broken

shards exquisitely weathered.

YES IN THE SENSE OF NO

This orange beach lies like a long tongue

longing for some other tongue to twist together

swells of words surging over slow vacillations

between *yes* and *no* spilling onto this canvased land,

desalinating distances between you and me and then.

And between the stones and junk of this former town dump,

lie half buried promises in hard-packed sand

bursting out jelly jar prisms, fragments of filtered sun

scattered through shattered necks of busted beer bottles,

loosed strands of cubic zirconia, the light

shredded, complete, remembered

the way last embraces linger between silhouetted lips

pulling back, pulling in, these waves, this sand.

IN SITU

This stone's heft flattens
the whites between my words,
pools there, still, like old water
just before the splash. Memory, too,
reads through this shell of rock,
this name. Pangea, a mountain seed,
delivered through these molted sands,
swaddled now within my palm,
a kindled breath released then caught.

... SUCH IS THE DUTY OF THE ARTIST

Heartbreak requires no hesitation,
no thought, just attention
carelessly everywhere breaking
beneath footprints sanded down
by the tips of memory's fine grit.

Weathering, too, needs no planning,
only commitment to touch—
a wounded tongue's addiction
to a ragged tooth's caresses—
sharp convictions, a stubborn will.

LEAVING RAIN

The rain has forgotten how to stop
falling, even how to fall—falling up,
falling through, falling back in on itself,
lost—the way your mother's empty eyes
look through you, to you. I hope it didn't
dog you the whole way to California.
Sometimes, everyone needs to leave
behind the rain, if only to dry out
habits, breathe in something else
besides water and this town's pulp.

North Beach, that last salmon run, left us both
cold, wet, even in the sun. Skunked. Like us.
I said *damn fish, broke, water, line, god, shit.*
You said *Chinook, water, diamonds, god, god.*
We couldn't figure it out, so you left
halfway to Spring. Funny how words act
as doorways rather than doors themselves.
Yours led you to oranges. Why can't I
follow where glass is just another word
for sand made too hot to remember its name?

Is there a word in California for *water,*
for the way it sounds when it beads
off my hat, dribbles down my shoulders,
seeps into my pockets, pooling inside canvas
and me, the way your hands once pulled together
inside mine like night holding in evening's last glow?
You used to hold onto the rain. And me.
Was anything ever there to really let go?
I wish I was the one who drove you
to California, oranges, and leaving rain.

ROADSIDE ATTRACTION IN POULSBO, WASHINGTON

A one hump camel comes from Egypt.
A two hump camel comes from Asia.
How ever did either wake up here,
humps soaked to the fat, and wide-eyed,
facing the most ugly, malformed camel
each had ever seen? How many years passed
with rain raining and raining and raining
before they stopped resenting the missing
or additional hump? How many teeth
hide inside their hides? How many scars?
I can't tell now; mud from this road-side nativity
coats both sets of thinning teeth and balding bellies.

After years without thirst, chewing their cud,
waiting for the return of magicians, manger kings,
mirages, do they ever wonder if this might not be
the right place? They've been places,
seen things, learned to enjoy
cotton candy, peanuts, the slow,
plump hands of little boys, girls.
And though they longed for the opposite sex,
they seemed contented to wait
not thinking of humps, but of sand,
dry sand, and long, slow days
sifting between oases.

HE WALKS ALONE UPHILL PONDERING GRAVITATIONAL WAVES

His breath conspires with this hill's uphill will,
rasps like the ridges composing this town's sky.
The bob of his umbrella directs the frame
through which he sees his hard boots against pavement,
rooftop pitches, water pooling down curbside troughs,
vanes tilting with old winds, the broken legs of flamingo lawn art,
and the concrete's glint beneath the water's slow motion film—
a documentary of his day, its end, in the making.

He takes a breath, grips tighter his canopy, and regards
the slope of pavement sweeping with it sprays of distant traffic
down into the surf foaming at the town's heels. He is alone

except for the rain. The rain. A villain
for so many complainers in need of villains—
little does this crowd know or care that the rain does not
lash, does not beat, does not drub, does not drum,
does not strike or storm, gavel or pelt.
It does not "impinge upon the earth"
or anything else. Like all of us
it simply falls. It's the one thing we have the ability
to begin with surprise, even at an age, this move
from not falling to falling. In this moment,
there is no letting go, no betweening. Just states
changed. A bud. A bloom. Opened then pressed
between pages until they themselves become
pages attending memory, gathered like funeral mourners.

Above my desk, the rain coats my window
like the many lies my younger self tells to me still:
Tomorrow you can have apples. And on occasion,
I've bitten into one of the many I've squirrelled away
only to find I've lost the taste among Newton's bones.

Against the shattered cliffs, evening gulls cast
empty promises into the late glow, feeding
that dying flame the way I keep time
by depositing my days and thoughts
into bank accounts. Retire? I tire over again and again,
tracing the curves smirching the bottom of my student's
military white essay, sounding out my own excuse:
I did not choose this theme.

And behind the rain-stained window pane,
I see the ridges magnified and broken.
What is climbing if not a momentary fall itself
from falling, that raindrop grace of clarity,
knowing all along the story, once begun ends
like all endings, in silent punctuation.

Somewhere, across the Olympic mountaintops,
autumn families gather inside an apple orchard,
toasting apple bread spread heavy with apple butter,
drunk down with apple spice and wine,
savoring all and each slice of their apple time.

THE RED SEASON

I.

I want to learn about color, so I climb
shoulders that know a thing about hue,
and lean into gray ridges leaning their lean shadows
darkly against crooked pines, firs, wild rosebuds,
and slope my way into swayback saddles,
down to that place where light cuts through
wind and rock and leaf and limb
with such fragile hands, it shatters
red cedar bark, silver fir,
scatters the shards like diamond flames
blown amongst the Beargrass and Bunchberry,
melting the wide mountain meadow sea
—Flett's Violet, Coralroot, Avalanche Lily,
Juniper, Pyrola, White Rhododendron—
all wax and twist and run together
cooling into the Gray Wolf River flow,
oozing past Indian Paint Brushes, the fingers
dragging the wind, painting red the storm
storming inside the closed wild rose and you.

I want to learn about gods, so I climb
shoulders that know nothing of men
or you, and plant hand above hand
into cracks and crevices, culling the high rock outcrops
formed from sand and mud and time,
where the fine, hard grit gripping my fingertips
is everything about to let go.
At six thousand feet and hanging from the side of a rib
up is everywhere, and down
still a long way to fall.

I want to learn what to learn, so I climb
shoulders that know nothing about gods
or men, and find ice: falls of ice falling
over an ice river clinging along
long lateral moraines running barren,
draped across the valley head
where the slow process of weathering
and rock and soil creep
have long since erased our marks.

II.

Here, the trail runs cold
up the mountain or down.
Here, in the broken slate,
the rocks are folded,
and the beds and folds
along the many small faults
have been pulled apart
like us. Everywhere
in the rounded knobs and ridges,
in the succession of sandstone and shale,
uplifted or folded,
erosion reveals patterns
of things now broken.

And here, at the end,
in the evening's darkness,
I pull out from within my coat pocket
a single, closed wild rose,
and in the heated palm of my open hand
the bud unfolds itself like a fortune lost
and won with each petal splayed,
its colors divided by red shadows
falling across this hued path
of boulder, pine, and sky.

Previously appeared in JACK SPENSER - Prism Book Number 3 (21st Editions. Ed. John Wood. 2011)

Author Intro

HEIDI HANSEN

At an early age, I learned the power of words. Given an option, I will always choose an essay test over True/False. In college I edited the weekly newspaper.

During my marketing career, I used words to fulfill requirements, but playing them into stories poking fun at everyday issues is my delight. It nearly got me fired when it fell into the wrong hands, but even then, it did not curb my appetite for writing. Being able to describe with enthusiasm helped me when I ventured into owning and operating a gift basket business catering to Silicon Valley high tech companies; then later as a Realtor in Sequim.

In the past few years, I've turned my attention once again to writing, taking classes, attending seminars and honing the craft in writing and critique groups. Along with Linda B. Myers, we founded the Olympic Peninsula Authors organization to help local authors get their works out in front of the public.

In 2016, I published a book of my short stories, titled *A Slice of Life* and followed up the next year with *A Second Slice*. I am honored to have one of my longer stories in this anthology.

Heidi is one of the hosts for the monthly open mic event in Sequim for writers, and the monthly Spontaneous Writing. Her books are available in print and eBook format on Amazon.com unless you happen upon the Olympic Peninsula Authors booth on any sunny Saturday.

CIVIL DISOBEDIENCE

Hazel tsk'd her teeth as she sorted through the mail in her mailbox. When she removed the electric bill and what looked like an invitation, an ad for toupees fluttered to the ground. She kicked at it with disdain. The breeze picked up the four-color advertisement and floated it across the street where it collided with a pine tree, and landed on a high bough, wedged against the trunk. She shoved the rest of the items in the mailbox to the rear and slammed the lid shut. She headed back up the driveway to the house, shaking her head. *Why won't they cease delivering things to my mailbox that are not specifically addressed to me?*

That was in the fifth year of her civil disobedience. It started the year after Everett left. She gathered up the wrongful mail and marched into the post office, setting the two-foot square box on the counter.

"First class or overnight?" the clerk asked but when she raised her head and looked at the box, she realized it was unsealed. "Oh my, that is not going to do. You must seal it."

"I'm returning it to you," Hazel stated. "This is not my mail."

Alice Clifford, the postal matron, stood on her tiptoes and peered into the box. She selected one sealed envelope and read aloud, "One thirty-two Chestnut Street. That is not your address?"

"No, it is my address. I am Hazel Williams, but it is not addressed to Hazel Williams, is it?"

"No, it says Mr. Everett Williams. Is that your husband?"

"No."

"Well, did Mr. Williams ever live at this address?"

"Of course, he did. But he doesn't anymore."

"He should have put in a change of address."

"Don't get me started on what he should have done. But he didn't."

The two women, each being in their mid-fifties, with tight perms, stood about five feet tall and locked glares.

Alice broke the stare. "Here, fill out this change of address form."

Hazel took the form and removed the pen from her pocketbook. "Wait, this asks for a forwarding address."

"Yes, we need to know where to send the mail if he is no longer at that address."

"I've got no idea where he is."

"Then you can't forward his mail."

Hazel shoved the incomplete form across the counter. Alice took it and tossed it into the garbage. Hazel turned to leave.

"Wait, you have to take this with you." She closed the flaps and pushed the box back to Hazel.

"I told you, he doesn't live there. I don't want his mail ... and another thing I don't want any mail that is addressed to occupant, or resident, or neighbor, or some such. From now on, I only will accept mail that is addressed to Hazel Williams and that's that." She slapped her hands together, turned and marched triumphantly from the post office.

"Wait . . ." called Alice, but Hazel was already out the door.

Alice carried the box of returned mail to the postmaster's office and set it on his desk. It could sit there until his return. He could decide what to do about it.

His resolution caused the ensuing eruption. He had the route carrier deliver all the mail in the box back to one thirty-two Chestnut Street. It would not all fit in the mailbox, so the carrier knocked on the door. Hazel peered out the window and seeing the postal carrier with her box in hand, refused to go to the door. He left a notice of mail to be picked up at the post office.

No new mail was delivered to her overflowing mailbox. Each day a new pale orange slip was taped to her door.

When there were six such notices, Hazel stormed into the post office and demanded to speak with the person in charge. Alice breathed a sigh of relief and advised Lyle Murray that a customer wanted to speak with him.

Lyle pushed his chair back from his desk and rose to his full height of five feet six-and-one-half inches and puffed out his chest, proud of his position in Little Gap. He was the highest-ranking government employee within a hundred miles.

"How may I help you?" he asked Hazel. He thrust out his hand introducing himself, "I am Lyle Murray, Postmaster."

Hazel placed the six notices in his hand.

He looked down, dismissed the items to Alice at the counter. "I, uh, I thought I was needed here."

"I want this to stop," Hazel said. "You seem to be the one in charge, you should be able to stop it."

"Stop what?" he asked.

"Your people keep delivering mail to me that I don't want."

"I'm sorry. We only deliver what is addressed to you."

"No, you don't. I told her last week that I wouldn't accept any mail not addressed to Hazel Williams at one thirty-two Chestnut Street and I returned all that you had been delivering that wasn't addressed to me."

"But . . ."

"And now the carrier won't deliver any mail to me because you have gone and stuffed the mailbox full of all this . . . this . . . this shit!"

"Calm down, I am sure we can resolve this." Lyle looked around, and realized that while Hazel had been talking several customers had entered the foyer and were listening. They were listening intently. "Let's go to my office and see if we can straighten this out."

One of the listeners, a man in a green jacket, piped up. "No, I want to hear how you are going to help Hazel. I got the same problem." His comment was followed by nods and "yes's" from several other patrons.

Hazel looked around. The man in the green jacket, a woman dressed in lavender from head to toe, a man and woman wearing matching t-shirts that had some message printed on them and a handful of others were now involved in her conversation. They seemed to be in full support of her plea and in fact wanted the same thing she did.

Hazel said, "I just want what is due me and none of this other stuff."

"Well, that is not exactly how the US Postal Service works."

"Let me get this straight. The US Postal Service is part of the government . . . " said the woman in lavender.

"Yeah, that is we the government, the government of the people . . . " said the husband in the matching t-shirt.

"And we're the people and we want our mail and no more. You can keep all these ads and spams," finished his wife. "Quit stuffing our mailboxes."

Lyle reached in his pocket and pulled out a handkerchief. He wiped the sweat from his upper lip and brow. This was not a job for the Postmaster, this should have been handled by Alice. He needed to extricate himself from this before it turned into a mob scene. "I'm sorry, but that is the way it is. You could have your mail delivered here to a post office box and then as you open the box, you can recycle any unwanted mail into the recycle bins placed there in the lobby."

"That's an inconvenience. I have a perfectly fine mailbox at my house," Hazel said. With the support of these other patrons, she continued. "And another thing, as my government agency, you should be obliged to meet the needs of your customers and not keep telling us you can't do what we want."

"Yeas" erupted from the crowd and a spattering of applause.

Lyle glared at Alice, "You should have handled this."

Alice shrugged. "If it was up to me, I'd stop delivering all the bulk rate mail."

"Then I'd have to fire you," Lyle said.

A standoff followed. The post office refused to deliver any mail to Hazel because her mailbox was full. They would not agree to her request to not deliver mail unless it was specifically addressed to her.

Hazel went into town and purchased the biggest mailbox they had at the Co-Op, and nailed it to the post in place of her current box. She sorted through all the mail that was in the old mailbox. Everything addressed to Everett went into the box to be returned to the post office, and she tossed everything else into the recycle bin.

She read up on her rights. If the post office delivered it to her and it didn't have her name, Hazel Williams, on it, she could do with it what she wanted, but if it had been mis-delivered and had someone else's name, she must return it to the post office.

As she sorted through the advertisements, catalogs, and seemingly important mail that was addressed to no one in particular, she shook her head. *All of us trying to save the planet and recycling and not causing waste, look at this,* she thought.

Who would ever think I was interested in a welding tool catalog? Or who in their right mind would send a Victoria Secret's catalog to a fifty-nine-year-old woman? It is all absurd. She stopped. Here was a problem. The AARP card was addressed to Hazel Shicklebaum, her maiden name. She hadn't used that name in thirty-five years. Some computer somewhere was spewing out address labels and slapping them on everything. Did they make enough money on this wide-spread distribution? They might as well be dropping it from planes onto whole neighborhoods. Why had the post office been suckered into delivering all this crap? Someone had to put a stop to it.

She set up a lawn chair next to the new mailbox and waited for the postal carrier.

Frances Miller pulled onto Chestnut Street whistling a tune until he saw Hazel in her lawn chair. He considered his options. Today was Tuesday, the day when he delivered the full color grocery store circulars to every mailbox on the route. He and Hazel had been around and around on her demands and he stood his ground, but it left him feeling queasy. He took the job because he liked the interaction with his route customers, he liked the people in Little Gap. Now he dreaded delivery to some, some like Hazel who had started tossing mail back at him. It was not his decision to deliver those ads, it was headquarters that made those deals.

Slowly he advanced down Chestnut Street to where Hazel was lying in wait for him. "Good day Hazel," he said cheerily through the open window of the mail truck.

"Good day Frances," she said. "Did you see the new mailbox? All cleaned out."

Frances looked at the mailbox, three times larger than the previous one. "I've got some mail for you."

"You know my terms," she said.

"It's not like I don't want to oblige, but I must do what my employer says."

"It's Tuesday, Frances. The garbage truck comes by at two, you deliver at one, so I'll leave the garbage can right here. You put the mail that's addressed to "Hazel Williams" in the mailbox and everything else you deliver to the nice blue recycle bin." She patted the box.

"I can't do that. It's against federal law to tamper with the mail. I can only put the mail into your mailbox or hand deliver to you." He dropped the grocery store flyers into her lap and accelerated to the next stop.

That afternoon, she took down the mailbox and installed a horizontal plank then re-installed the new bigger mailbox and the old smaller mailbox. She painted on the side of the old mailbox "Hazel Williams" and "All Other" on the new one. Satisfied she waited for the next mail delivery.

She watched from inside the house, not wanting to intimidate him. Frances got out of the mail truck and studied the two mailboxes. There was nothing in the handbook about a patron having more than one box for delivery. He sorted through the handful of mail that he had and put the two envelopes clearly marked with Hazel's name into the old mailbox and everything else, including one addressed to Everett Williams into the "Other" box. He thought that she had come up with the perfect solution. Now they both could be happy.

Bill White who lived across the street from Hazel came over and investigated why she now had two mailboxes for one thirty-two Chestnut Street. He walked up to number two forty-six and told them how Hazel had installed an "other" box for mail not specifically addressed to her.

Virginia Jorgensen cocked her head and thought about it. "Well, I'll be, that's a fine idea."

Frances noted that two days later two forty-six Chestnut Street now had two mailboxes and within a week, every home on Chestnut Street had followed suit. Bill White offered to lend a hand with the installations as needed. When Frances returned to the post office after a long day of double-box deliveries, he was asked why it was taking him longer to do his route. Rather than tell his supervisor about the double mailboxes, he thought he would cover for Hazel and the patrons on Chestnut Street hoping they would tire of the mailboxes and all would return to normal. Although with Hazel, he wasn't sure what normal looked like.

Virginia told her bridge group how she had cut out all the spam mail.

"I think it is brilliant," said Betty. She pulled out her cell phone and called her husband. "While you are at the Co-Op will you buy another mail box?"

Chuck was at the check-out counter when Betty called. He said "sorry" to the clerk and went in search of a mailbox. "She must have mowed down the one we had when she backed out of the driveway today," he said placing it on the counter.

"We sure have been selling a lot of mailboxes lately," said the clerk.

"Has there been a rash of wives taking them out?"

"No, it's got something to do with the other mail."

"What do you mean?"

"Well, everyone is installing two mailboxes now and instructing the mail carrier to deliver mail addressed to them by name in one, and to put everything else into the other."

"What did you say?" The man standing in line behind Chuck asked.

The clerk explained about the two boxes to him, then to the people behind him in line. Each time she explained, she sold another mailbox.

That week, The Daily Comet which was actually a weekly, carried a front-page story about how the Co-Op sold out of mailboxes the previous week and wanted customers to know that they were taking orders and additional stock would be on the shelves by the end of the month. On the editorial page, there were three letters posting "raves" to the post office for offering this "other" service to patrons. There was one rant from Will Jackson who wrote that the post office should be offering the "other" service to customers who were paying for their post office boxes and getting them all jammed up with ads, not just first-class mail.

The following week, the postmaster sat for an interview with the local radio station. His superior at the state capital had instructed him that the amount of overtime being billed by his carriers due to the other mailboxes would not be tolerated. That was what he was supposed to say, but from the get go, he received high praise and compliments about the ingenious solution. He blustered with pride and never said that they would no longer service the other mailboxes.

Bob Hansen, a reporter looking for his next story of interest was driving his family to the lake for the weekend. Planning on fishing, he stopped in Little Gap for gas and went into the Co-Op to get a local fishing license. He saw the neon pink sign on the front door.

Mailboxes are OUT OF STOCK
pre-order TODAY
next order due FRIDAY

At the counter, he asked the clerk what that was all about.

A few minutes later, his wife and three kids trailed into the store looking for him.

"Oh there you are, what's taking so long?" his wife asked. The kids had questions of their own.

"Daddy, can we go fishing now?" said a boy of about ten.

"I have to go pee," said a girl in a pink and white checked dress.

"Can I get a candy?" asked another boy with red hair, stuffing salt-water taffy into his pockets. "I'm starving."

"Gladys, take the kids. I've got a story here." He turned back to the clerk. "Are there any locals I could interview about this?"

"You can ask anyone. Everyone seems to be in on it now. That's why we had to put that sign up."

A man in paint-splattered overalls interrupted them. "Mindy, where'd you put the mailboxes?"

"Hank, can't you read the sign? We are sold out. More coming Friday."

Bob turned to Hank and asked," I'm doing a story about the mailboxes and wondered if we could talk?"

"Nothing to talk about, I need a mailbox."

As Bob left the Co-Op, the clerk hollered after him, "It all started over on Chestnut Street."

Back in the car, Bob told his family. "We've got a quick little diversion before we go to the lake. Where the hell is the map? We need to find Chestnut Street."

It might have stopped there, but two events collided in the town of Little Gap on Wednesday. Bob Hansen got the byline of his lifetime when his human-interest story about the other mailboxes got picked up by USA Today and The New York Times. Reporters from every possible news source descended on the town to cover the story. Their vans rolled onto Chestnut Street and the photographers set up their tripods. Video was rolling when the FBI pulled into Hazel

Williams' driveway. When their black SUV with tinted windows came to a stop, all four doors opened simultaneously. Reporters stopped midsentence and advanced on the vehicle and motioned for their cameramen to point their lenses at one thirty-two Chestnut Street. Something big was going down.

When the doors opened, four men dressed in dark suits wearing Ray Ban sunglasses stepped out and walked to the front door.

"Just like *Men In Black,* Bill White said.

"They got guns," another neighbor said.

When the doorbell rang, Hazel looked out and saw a mob of neighbors gathering in her front yard. They were trampling down the early shoots in her flowerbeds. She was ready to shoo them away, only the four ominous men at her door distracted her.

"Hazel Williams?" one man asked.

"Yes," she said.

"We are with the Federal Bureau of Investigation and we are here to arrest you."

"Arrest me? For what?"

"For tampering with the mail."

"What are you talking about?"

"It has come to our attention that you have been obstructing mail delivery. Ma'am you do realize that is a federal offense?"

"What?"

"Punishable by law," he continued. "You have been reported taking mail not addressed to you and disposing of it illegally. Is that true?"

"If anything, I have been doing the exact opposite. Look at my mailboxes." She stepped onto the porch and pointed.

"One is for my mail and the other one is for everything else the post office delivers to me."

All four men turned and followed her pointed finger. One of the FBI agents trotted to the mail boxes. Bill White reported that he appeared to take photos with a small camera posing as a tie clip.

"Ma'am, and what do you do with the mail in that big box marked 'Other'?"

"I return it to the post office."

"What?" It was his turn to question. "Our reports indicate that you are tossing mail not specifically addressed to your person into the garbage."

"That is against the law," a second man in a black suit said.

"I know that. That's why I keep returning it to the post office," Hazel said exasperated.

"What about mail addressed to Everett Williams?"

"Any mail addressed to him and all mail not addressed to me."

"They're arresting Hazel?" Bill White shouted.

"Naw, looks like they are just talking to her," Virginia's husband said.

"Free Hazel," Bill shouted, "Free Hazel!"

He said it two or three times, but the mob picked up on it and soon it was a loud chant. Neighborhood dogs began to howl, crows cawed and someone dialed 9-1-1. Feed from the reporters was already uploading to their out-of-town editors before the local sheriff arrived on Chestnut Street. News stories of the mob scene and Free Hazel campaign were breaking in on the afternoon broadcast television stations across the nation.

All this coverage led to in-depth conversations about what constituted mail and the legal aspects of what you could and could not toss without breaking the law. Ads for dual mailboxes filled the airways, but the question was what to do with the stuff in the other mailbox.

In another interview with the postmaster of Little Gap, Lyle Murray, admitted that Hazel Williams would bag up her other mail and return it to the post office whenever the mailbox got full. His discussions with her never resolved the problem so he put it in a storeroom but after five years of returns, the storeroom was full, and it wasn't just Hazel returning unwanted mail anymore. In fact, Little Gap had to install new receptacles at the station which were clearly marked "RETURNED MAIL ONLY." Because there was mail that was first class and addressed to individuals like Everett Williams who had no forwarding address, these items needed to be marked "undeliverable" or "refused" and returned to the sender. Unless there was no return address, in which case, it would be held in the dead letter office. Due to the double mailboxes at every address, the carriers had to sort and stuff at each address. This added so much labor that there had not been time to sort through the returned mail and ferret out what could be forwarded or what had to be returned. A once-abandoned warehouse on the other side of town was now filling up with returned mail.

When the fervor reached its pitch, there was a conference at Post Office Headquarters in Washington DC. The Postmaster General dropped the gavel calling the meeting to order.

"This has gotten totally out of hand," he said. "I have here a stamp commissioned by Congress that they are about to print. It is a Free Hazel stamp. I cannot allow this."

"We are no longer able to sort all the incoming mail and the returned mail," reported one of the men seated at the conference table.

"We need to raise rates," said the delegate from accounting.

"The President of the United States wants a statement from us. She is going live tonight and needs this uprising squelched."

"It's not just us, it's happening all over the world, the UK, France, even Switzerland."

"Wherever deals have been cut to deliver advertisements."

"But that is how we make ends meet," said marketing. "If only we could find a way to get a cut on email . . ."

". . . and tweets . . ."

The meeting broke into laughter.

"How did this get started?"

Everyone exchanged questioning looks, and shrugs.

"Who is Hazel Williams?" A voice called out.

More laughter.

"Who is John Galt?"

No one was sure who asked that question.

That night in a press conference, the President of the United States reported that the government's postal system was being revamped and would outsource all mail handling to UPS and FedEx. Henceforth the Post Office would only issue stamps. She continued that she was pleased to announce the issuance of the Free Hazel stamp.

The next day, mailboxes on eBay were a dime a dozen.

Author Intro

JAN THATCHER ADAMS, MD

I practiced womb to tomb family medicine for twenty-five years before becoming an ER doctor at Olympic Medical Center. Through the years, I authored scores of published articles as well as my autobiographical book *Football Wife: Coming of Age with the NFL*. It chronicles my marriage to a football hero during the wild early days of the NFL.

I landed in Port Angeles after viewing the beautiful town and its setting from the Black Ball ferry, crossing the Strait from Victoria. I got off the boat, drove west and bought a plot of land on Freshwater Bay. There I built a home, but as plans have a way of derailing, it would be eighteen years before I moved here full time, after a near lifetime of battling Minnesota mosquitoes and ticks. I live here now with my actor/director husband and three cats.

My poems in this anthology were written in the years when a woman doctor was a rarity and much less medical technology was available.

The autobiography by Jan Adams, *Football Wife: Coming of Age with the NFL*, was published in 2011 and is available on Amazon.com.

DREAMS
IN THE SERVICE OF WHOLENESS

She knew her death approached. She knew the cancer would kill her. After all, she'd been an army nurse, working in the Veterans' Hospital for 30 years after the war. And the doctors at Mayo Clinic, though they administered radiation and powerful chemotherapy, were quite blunt with her--the treatments were only for improving her quality of life for a time. They would not save her.

But she had developed quite an ability for denial. So every time I tried to discuss her impending death with her, she would not hear me. She would not check her will, say her good-byes, or put in order any undone words or deeds. Her denial was stronger than her body. Though her condition deteriorated, necessitating nursing home placement, she continued to deny her mortality.

Then one day she noticed a newspaper article about some dream classes I was teaching for the local Community Education. The next time I visited her, she began a conversation.

"I saw the article about you," she said. "Do you know how to interpret dreams?"

"Yes," I told her. "Why? Do you have a dream to share?"

"Well," she began, "I had this dream the other night. It was so vivid, I can still see it in front of my eyes. It was beautiful, but I wonder what it means."

"Well, tell me about it," I said.

"I dreamt I was taking a plane trip, up into the blue sky in a shimmering white Concorde, to Paris. I got to the door of the plane, where I was met by the captain. The pilot was a white-haired gentleman in sparkling white uniform. I can still see the epaulets on his shoulder. He seemed almost to glow in the whiteness of his uniform and the outside of the plane."

"When he gestured for me to step inside, I noticed there were no other passengers. 'Oh, I said, I'm not going to go on this trip. It's too wasteful to have this elegant plane trip just for me.'"

"The pilot said, 'Yes you are.'"

"I looked again into the interior of the plane and saw a luscious dinner all set for my pleasure. Again, I said, 'Well, I'm not going on this trip. I've not been eating much lately, and it would be wasteful to have that meal just for me.'"

"The pilot said, 'Yes you are.'"

"Once more, I looked into the luxurious interior of the plane, and noticed a bottle of fine wine, champagne, perhaps, opened and ready to pour into a fine crystal glass. So, I said, 'I'm not going on this trip. I can't drink any alcohol lately. It doesn't agree with my stomach any more. I don't want such a fine bottle of wine wasted.'"

"The pilot said, 'Yes you are."

"Oh," she said, "it was such a wonderful, beautiful dream. It makes me feel warm and calm all over. What do you suppose it means?"

At this, a look traveled between her eyes and mine. In that way, it was understood that she knew perfectly well what the dream meant. Sharing the dream in this way with me was her way of informing me she was making peace with the process, and was at least doing some of the inner work so critical for that last phase of life.

So, I answered her question in a general sort of way, encouraging her to draw her own conclusions. "Well," I said, "think about the action of the dream. You are going to take a trip into the sky, ushered by a glowing gentleman of extraordinary kindness, transported in a vehicle of surpassing comfort and peace. You are resisting this trip, but the gentleman is quietly insistent, despite your protests. Remember that all dreams come to you in the service of wholeness. I believe this dream has a gentle, reassuring message you will not ignore."

She smiled slightly at this, then changed the subject.

Not long after this discussion, she slipped into a coma, then died. What a gift this dream had been, what a reassurance, what an answer to her fears.

Over the years, my patients have related countless dreams to me. They invariably prove useful in the whole creative stewpot called healing. Sometimes they point to therapeutic ideas, sometimes to source conflicts that figure in the dis-ease process. Often they provide laughter, always they reconnect with wonder and mystery.

Occasionally they are predictive.

One of the most common sort of dream occurs during pregnancy, and often is about having twins, or about some characteristic of the baby growing in the womb. Most of the time, these dreams are not predictive, but reflect in some way the anxieties or hopes or state of mind of the mom-to-be.

In the same way, dreams about death are often reported to me. Such dreams are rarely about actual death, but reflect huge transformation taking place either with the person in the dream or with some aspect of the dreamer the dream subject represents. But once, such a dream foretold a tragedy.

A first-time mom, in late pregnancy, awoke terrified from a dream that her baby had died. In the middle of the night, frightened, she called her relative who works on the maternity unit.

The relative urged her to come in for some fetal monitoring, to reassure her. The monitoring was entirely normal, and she went back home to bed. A few days later, I saw her in the office, and she told me this story. We listened to the baby's heartbeat, and noticed several vigorous, reassuring kicks.

Then, a few days later, she presented to the maternity ward with ruptured membranes. Though she was four weeks early, I was not concerned, as most babies do fine when delivered just a bit early. But my unconcern changed to grief when no fetal heart tones could be found. She was in labor, all right, but it had started because the baby was dead.

And so, in dream work, as in life, there are no absolutes. In this one case, the rule about death in dreams not representing actual death was broken.

It is sometimes difficult to see how such a dream and how such a tragedy can come to lives in the service of wholeness. But the grieving process caused the young woman to examine and discharge some unfinished baggage from her teen years, baggage preventing her from a full enjoyment of her life.

Last week, it was my huge privilege and pleasure to deliver a lusty, vibrant, beautiful baby boy for this same young woman and her husband. Their joy was palpable throughout the maternity ward.

Dreams, in the service of wholeness, and Time, in the service of healing, join hands as powerful medicine, gifts from the gods. In my doctor's bag, they are indispensable.

IN MACEDONIA WITH PATCH ADAMS

In northern Macedonia, a bus moves along the heat-shimmering modern highway, weaving in traffic of heavy trucks and horse-drawn farm wagons. In the fields, farm families scythe hay in alfalfa liberally sprinkled with orange poppies, and horse-drawn plows ply the earth. White homes with red roofs make stunning contrasts against the distant snow-covered mountains and chaparral.

Suddenly, the bus turns on to a dirt road, and the scenery abruptly changes to an endless vista of white and army-green tents, chain-link fence, and long lines of bedraggled people, holding children and bundles. This oddly uniform landscape is the measure and scope of home for those who have escaped the atrocities of Kosovo. One of several camps in the area, this one is currently receiving several thousand new refugees who crossed the border in the last twenty-four hours.

When the bus opens its doors, a choking cloud of dust billows in, and the doors are quickly closed. In a few moments, the dust settled, a kaleidoscopic patchwork of color and silliness spills from the bus, for Patch Adams and his clown friends have arrived, ready to clown in some of the most difficult circumstances currently on the planet.

Patch, the subject of the popular 1998 movie "Patch Adams," has for many years traveled with his clown friends to trouble spots of the world, such as Russia and Bosnia. Most of us have left busy lives for this trip, and have come on short notice. All of us have a deep commitment to the idea and the reality that humor, even in the worst of events, can and does have powerful healing effects. And we all understand that the large-scale human disaster of the Kosovars is a circumstance of endless personal tragedy.

We show our identification permits to the Macedonian police guarding the camp entrance. They ask us all, despite our brilliant clown clothes and paint, what our purpose is in coming there. Once inside, we wade in to a crowd of amazed children and weary mothers and life-stunned fathers and heart-sore grandparents. We have all been in difficult places before, but never when the wounds are so very fresh, the bleeding so recent, the loss so complete and uniform.

For the next three days, we are witness to the power of laughter. The children are nearly hysterical with glee, and we are swept along in a tide of thousands who wish and hope only for a touch, a smile, a kiss, a hug, a silly gesture. It is nearly impossible to clown in any kind of traditional way, as we are each surrounded by hundreds who tug, pull on arms, drag on clothes, goose, pinch, hug, and basically try to get as close as possible. With five children on each side holding hands with me, I wade on and on, reaching to kiss and connect with the babies held over the crowd by their parents who seek a blessing and baptism of laughter for their little ones.

One tall man in a faded jean jacket follows me wherever I am that first day. He doesn't say much to me, but is clearly happy to be participating in this pent-up burst of joyful energy. But eventually the crowd becomes dangerous—little children are at risk of trampling, and the older children become aggressive and unruly. I believe I will have to leave the area for a cooling off period. But suddenly, this tall man begins playing a tune on a plastic recorder, and the crowd responds with clapping hands and swaying bodies—and the situation is defused.

A young man explains to me that this tall man is not quite right in the head, but that he has a special gift—he is the camp Fool. He makes it his business to be always out about the camp. Whenever he encounters a tense situation, he manages to do something silly or fun or musical that completely calms everyone. And so, he is called The Doctor. The Doctor guards me every day I am in this camp, and I know I am in good hands.

We return each day to the same camp. With great regularity, bombs explode with loud dynamite thuds in nearby Kosovo, just two miles away. Each time, the clowning stops for a moment and the people cheer and shout NATO! NATO! Mothers explain to me how difficult it is for the children to sleep at night, when the bombs fall much more often.

We all hear endless stories of atrocities in Kosovo, told quietly with tearful eyes. We try to imagine the loss, and the effect on an entire culture of seeing friends and families routinely beaten with baseball bats, children and old folks' eyes gouged out, far pregnant women bayoneted in the bellies, homes looted and burned, and families and friends murdered in the most unspeakable ways.

In particular, these children in these camps have lost their childhood. Their artwork depicts gruesome documentaries of scenes from horribly exploded lives—guns and blood and graves and burning homes and tanks. Their bodies are still those of children, but their eyes tell another story—of a loss of innocence.

And so the clowns work and play to bring back the memories of that innocence, of a time when laughter and security and simple joys and family were the fabric of their existence. In a moment of deep connection, a thirty-year-old man thanks us for giving back these children their childhood. He explains everyone in camp has been worried because they have not smiled for months, they have become aggressive, and their eyes are so very old. "And now," he says, "they have the possibility of recovering their childhood. Please, come back again and again."

While Patch himself cannot come back over and over again in the next months, he has worked tirelessly to build a network of clowns around the world, and for years has asked them to be ready at any time to be ambassadors of joy when needed. So, there will be clowns in these camps! They will return every three weeks. And these children, who have enough food and are not cold or wearing rags, will also have the opportunity for ongoing nourishment and care of their little traumatized spirits.

THOMAS

Before colonoscopy was
the screening for colon cancer,
We doctors provided a draconian procedure
called proctoscopy.

The proctoscope, a 14 inch long steel tube, inflexible.
The examination — painful, done without sedatives,
on the bottom of my
Favorites in procedures.

Even so, it was needed.
So, Thomas presents himself,
after a long night of fun with laxatives.
To finish his prep, my nurse hands him two Fleet enemas.
She shows him to the bathroom.

My gleaming torture instrument awaits him
And waits
And waits
And waits.

Finally, my nurse knocks on the bathroom door.
"Is everything ok?"

"Well," he says," I drank both of them but nothing is
happening!"

Lucky man!
He has to reschedule his torture!

FRANKIE

Here he is again.
It is his monthly ER visit
For tooth pain.

At 26, his mouth is filled with black rotting
And cracked stumps for teeth.
This is the result of his relentless
Meth habit.

He has braved the deep snow and bitter cold,
Walking in the dawn hours from
His homeless shelter.

He is praying the doctor in the ER
Will give him oxy's for his tooth pain—
Of course it says right there on his chart
He is allergic to all narcotics, Tylenol, and ibuprofen—
Except OxyContin. This is the drug he can sell on the street
to get more meth.

He does not go to the dentist—
Despite the free clinic info
we provide him each month.
Tooth repair is not his goal.

It is a bad day for him.
He got me for his doctor.

I write him a prescription for antibiotic
to clean up his mouth.

No oxy
He is angry.

As I am leaving the room,
He turns and
Pees on the back wall of his exam room.

I do not comment.
Instead, I remind myself—
I have all his luck!

CHARLES

He was small, elderly, grumpy, crude and rude.
He abused the nurses verbally and with his cane.
His nightly 2 AM ambulance to ER visits never varied.

"I can't sleep, my back hurts, I haven't pooped
For 5 days!
Give me that f*****g shot, now!"
All attempts to divert him to non-narcotic
Medicines failed. His demands would be met,
Or he would not go home.
All information supplied him regarding the dangers of his
escalating narcotic use and constipation problems
Went unheeded.

One morning I arrived
for morning hospital rounds
To find him admitted,
with multiple enema treatments under way.

My examination revealed
an ominously hard, swollen belly,
With no bowel sounds.
I knew immediately he
Was on his last narcotic mission.

CT scan confirmed his ruptured bowel,
His abdomen filled with foul fluid.
Surgery was his only hope,
And likely to be the final event
Of his miserable, frail existence.

The surgery was a success.
Some days later, Charles died.

Sometimes, a strong and abusive
Personality
Leads to fatal consequences.

LARA AND TONYA

They are beautiful children, ages 5 and 7.

Their illnesses—mild colds.

They have a history of ear infection,

so mom brought them in.

Curly long hair, mischievous laughs,

And cheerful smiles inform me they are not

In serious medical trouble.

I notice their Russian names.

"Mom, are you Russian?" I ask.

5-year-old Lara interjects, "No. Mom loves Dr. Chicago!"

I never know where the next laugh will arise,

But I know for certain it will be healing.

Author Intro

VYKKI MORRISON

I am a Port Angeles resident with a passion for writing and art. Growing up surrounded by the magic of the Vermont hills, I found my muse early, and have been writing since the age of eight. Over the years I've moved around a bit, but in 2015 the lure of Washington called. My muse responded, finding joy and a home in the beautiful Washington countryside.

Vykki says her writing can be found in a number of venues in the States and Canada, including some very old refrigerator doors.

THE BLACKBERRY FESTIVAL

George sat on the ground and pulled on his size sixteen shoes before hauling himself up the ravine. He stepped over the guardrail and brushed himself off as best as possible. His clothes were dirty, so it didn't make much of a difference, but they were the only ones he had. He itched all over and did his best not to scratch. That would definitely keep people away, and he was determined to enjoy the festivities in Joyce, people included.

He himself was scruffy, an ugly man with a long beard and a shock of straw-like hair. The scientific name was Uncombable Hair Syndrome, a genetic thing that was rare and probably the only thing he'd ever have in common with Einstein. George was broad, both in the shoulders and everywhere else, and inordinately tall. He looked a little like the wrestler, Andre the Giant. He hoped his looks didn't scare children. Maybe, he thought, he should have dressed like a clown.

George set out for Joyce and the Blackberry Festival. He'd heard the Blackberry Café had incredible cinnamon buns, and a twenty-eight-ounce Sasquatch burger. It would have been George-size if he ate meat. He may look like he ate whole animals for breakfast, but he was a vegetarian. Which was going to make those blackberry pies even more special. His stomach was already rumbling.

The Joyce, WA Blackberry Festival happened every summer. Bands played old country music in front of the general store, and people danced if they could find room. It was always well attended, people coming from a distance to enjoy the experience of the music, the vendors and, of course, the blackberry pie contest. The fire department demonstrated a rescue in which they used the Jaws of Life on an unsuspecting wreck. Kids wore fire hats for the remainder of the festival.

George was excited. He'd wanted to attend the Festival for years, but something always prevented it. This year he was going to enjoy every moment. Ten minutes of walking brought him within range of music, an old Johnny Cash song. Another two minutes and he was passing the café. When he reached the general store, he dropped the torn backpack he'd been carrying in a dumpster and joined the crowd listening to music.

The next thing he did was to check out the pie. Moving up in the line, he was already salivating. A little lady, no taller than his thigh, waited on him. "Which one would you like, dear?" she asked.

He opened his mouth, then closed it quickly. His teeth were yellow, almost brown, and he didn't want anyone seeing. That's what happened when you lived in the woods without amenities like running water or a toothbrush, for that matter. It was embarrassing, so he just pointed.

"You're a big man. Let's see if we can't get you a larger piece, hmm?" She cut a generous wedge and handed him the plate with a smile. "That will be seven dollars. Enjoy that pie, now."

George dropped a ten on the table and found a place to sit while he ate. It *was* good pie, and he enjoyed every mouthful.

Next came dancing. He swayed and turned, almost bumping into a child who somehow ended up standing on top of his feet while he followed the tunes. The people around him stared and took pictures at the sight of the huge man and the tiny girl. He didn't notice. He was reveling in the experience.

After her parents called to her, George wandered over to watch the fire department's demonstration. It was interesting, but his attention kept being pulled to an exhausted mother and young boy who was jumping up trying to see. The boy tugged at her skirt, demanding "Mama, mama, pick me up." George thought she looked too tired to lift a feather, much less a child.

Looking down, he caught her eye and smiled, holding his arms out for the boy. The weary mother gave a relieved sighed and a whispered, "Thank you." George lifted the boy who happily watched the demo sitting on a broad shoulder, the best seat in the house.

When the demonstration ended, and after one last piece of pie, George headed out. The overhead sun said it was close to four, and the vendors were beginning to pack up. No use hanging around. Moving with long strides, he listened to music until he could no longer hear the band playing. Whether he was too far away, or they stopped playing, he didn't know. What he did know was just how much joy he felt from attending the festival. His ugly face broke into a grin, yellow teeth and all.

This would become one of his happiest memories, being around others, participating, able to enjoy children in an atmosphere of acceptance, no one scared of him or ostracizing him because of his unique looks. He'd lived a mostly solitary and anti-social existence due to his appearance, and while the busyness of the festival tired him out and made him feel a little claustrophobic, it was well worth it.

Soon enough he was at the ravine. Pulling himself over the guardrail again, he made it quickly to the bottom and slipped between the trees. At his encampment, he stripped off the size sixteen shoes and his 'good clothes' and put them away. Then he gave himself a good scratch all over, an accompanying grunt of relief, and went about his business. It was a good day.

Hours later, in the dark Joyce night, a man searched for food. Raising the lid on the dumpster he found something almost better. Someone had thrown a full knapsack in the garbage. It was filthy and it stunk, but it could be something. Unzipping it, he turned the bag upside down. Out fell a dozen empty cans of shaving cream, razors, and pounds of what smelled like wet dog hair. He gagged. If he didn't know better, he'd have said someone shaved a Sasquatch.

Author Intro

ABIGAIL JONES

I am eleven years old and in sixth grade. The subjects I look forward to during the day are Math and Bible. In my free time I like to sew, read, draw, and write. I love to swim as well. When I grow up, I hope to become either a business owner or an author. I wrote these poems to express my love for the wonderful place we live in that God created for us.

My favorite part about where I live is that you can be in the mountains and near the sea at the same time. I have written many poems, but have only published the two in this book. I love going to Salt Creek, where I can explore the tide pools and discover the crabs. I have lived on the Olympic Peninsula all of my life and I love the amazing views and places to go. My favorite places to go on the Peninsula are the Hoh Rainforest and Lake Crescent. I've gone camping at both places, and it was a very pleasant experience. I hope you like my poems.

MY HOME

Where the mountains meet the sea,
Where the deer run free,
That is where you'll find me.

Where the otters swim in the ocean all day,
Where the sky is pure blue, and the raccoons play,
That is where I will be.

Where the evergreens grow,
Where the wild geese go,
That is where I shall stay.

Where the gleaming sun shines bright,
Where frogs sing through the night,
That is where I will live.

This land is my home,
Where I will roam.
Yes, this is my place
Where the wild winds race,
Where the waves crash down with a thundering sound,
Where the eagle glides free,
Over rivers and trees.

Yes, this is my home,
Where I shall roam.
This is my place to be,
Where I can
run wild, be brave, and live free.

NIGHTFALL

A wild wind blows from the east to the west.

A robin feeds her chicks from a tangly nest.

A lonely wolf howls

While the cougar prowls.

And the owl calls "Who?"

As if somebody knew.

The fawn lays still

On a moonlit hill.

While the canaries make not a peep

In their dreamless sleep.

All of nature knows,

As the sunlight goes,

That night's coming in

As the darkness begins.

Bringing a wall of black over their shut eyes.

As the cold comes closer,

In their dreams the creatures hide.

Author Intro

LES CARNAHAN

I'm not sure how to explain my fascination with the history of World War II. I have studied the war for over two decades. My personal library is heavy with books from technical descriptions of the machinery of war, to personal eyewitness accounts and chronicles of journalists and historians. I devour them all with wonder and appreciation for the sacrifice, courage and devotion with which the war was fought.

After college, I joined the United States Air Force and graduated second in my class at Chanute AFB. I was assigned to the 9th Reconnaissance Squadron at Beal AFB, California, and worked on the SR-71 Black Bird, the U-2 Dragon Lady, and KC-135 tankers as well as T-38 Talon trainers as an Avionics Technician.

A career in education teaching grades 4 through 12 ended with my retirement in 2010. I continue to pursue self-education of all things that interest me.

I split my year between my homes in Port Angeles, Washington and Upland, California depending upon the time of year and of course, the most favorable weather.

Les can be followed on Facebook at Leslie Carnahan.

THE STRAIT OF JUAN DE FUCA INCIDENT

Pulling at the crotch of his uniform, Second Lieutenant Habersham was questioning the wisdom of requesting heavy starch from the laundry before embarking upon a long train trip from Ventura California to the Northwest. Now bumping along in the right front seat of a Dodge WC63 6 X 6 truck, borrowed from the Signal Corps for the trip from Fort Lewis to Camp Hayden, his discomfort was growing mile by mile.

"Crying out loud, Sergeant, have you hit every damn pothole in the road?"

"No Sir! I have missed a few but I'll try harder to get them all if you want." Staff Sergeant Gantry smirked.

"Not funny, Sergeant! My ass is sore, I'm tired, and I'll never see any action before this damn war is over."

"Sorry Sir, but I can't help but think there are a few thousand mugs who wish they were in your shoes."

That was probably true, the baby-faced lieutenant thought. But it was no comfort either physically or mentally to the young officer. Dale Habersham had waited impatiently to graduate from the University of California to join the Army and fight. The only son of a wealthy citrus grower in Ventura County, he had first been deferred from joining by age, and then because of his studies in engineering at the University of California. His family insisted that he complete college.

The war with Germany had been over for nearly a month, and the Japanese, after a bloody battle on Okinawa, had been driven back to their mainland and had been enduring heavy bombing by the Allies. The lieutenant had trained as an artillery spotter and was certain he would be part of the invasion force. Although he suspected his father may have had something to do with his current assignment because of political friends of the family, it had actually been an Army decision not to send an inexperienced officer into what was expected to be the bloodiest and most difficult battle of the war.

Battery 131 at Camp Hayden on the Olympic Peninsula was completed in May, 1945 and turned over to the Army the next month. It had been constructed as part of a series of shore batteries designed to protect shipping in the Strait of Juan De Fuca and the Puget Sound and most importantly, the naval bases there from Japanese warships. Battery 131, consisting of two 16" long range naval guns mounted individually in concrete casements five-hundred feet apart, with an earth covered concrete corridor between them that housed crew and armament, was built at a cost of $1,557,500 taxpayer dollars. Each gun was capable of hurling a one-ton projectile nearly 28 miles.

Lt. Habersham had been trained on smaller Army Howitzers, but since he was an artillery spotter, it really didn't matter what he was spotting for, so the Army felt him qualified for the post. Lt. Habersham had wanted nothing more than to fight but was now realizing it wasn't going to happen at Camp Hayden. He was not looking forward to this assignment.

After miles of green forest and glimpses of the Hood Canal and Strait of Juan De Fuca, the lieutenant had envisioned Camp Hayden as a collection of tents in the woods, with some of the artillery of the type he had seen at Army camps placed near the water's edge. He had not been briefed about what sort of guns he would be spotting for. As the big Dodge bounced to a halt in front of what looked like a concrete entrance to a cave, his preconceived visions evaporated like the mist that swirled overhead.

"What the hell?" He stepped from the truck while the sergeant unloaded his duffle bag from the back of the truck. "This is it?"

Emerging from the entrance was a corporal in wrinkled fatigues that looked even younger than the lieutenant. The corporal picked up the lieutenant's duffle, then dropped it and snapped to a crooked salute.

"Corporal Grant, Sir! Welcome to Camp Hayden."

"Thank you, Corporal, how about not dropping my duffle too many times O.K.?"

"No Sir! Yes Sir! Please follow me Sir!"

The corporal picked up the duffle, this time securely and headed for the entrance. Lt. Habersham followed into the wide doorway past a humming generator and into a well-lit but stark looking hallway. They walked past stacks of white, cloth-covered cylinders that reminded him of base drums covered in muslin. But the no smoking signs everywhere meant these were some sort of explosive. The lieutenant was puzzled by these. The artillery shells he was familiar with contained gun powder within the shell. He pointed at them not verbalizing his curiosity.

"Navy powder packs, Sir." Corporal Grant answered the lieutenant's unspoken question.

They entered a much larger hallway that was mostly empty except for about a dozen or so Army issue cots, some with sleeping gun crew members. They turned into a small office with not much more than a desk and a few chairs.

The corporal set the duffle bag down outside the door with exaggerated carefulness and gestured for the lieutenant to enter. Stepping inside, the lieutenant saw a major behind the desk writing on some sort of form, head down with an unlit cigar dangling from his mouth. The major looked to be in his fifties with salt and pepper hair closely cut. The lieutenant noticed a nameplate on the desk that identified the officer as Maj. Glen Dunney.

The lieutenant snapped to attention, "Lieutenant Habersham reporting for duty, Sir!"

"Take a seat lieutenant, I'll be with you in a second." The major scribbled a few more words, then appeared to sign the form with a flourish, letting out a shout which startled the lieutenant. "Sergeant Flint!"

A sergeant materialized seemingly out of thin air. "Yes Sir?"

"Duty roster for tonight." The major handed the form to the sergeant.

"Yes Sir." The sergeant scanned the duty sheet while glancing over at the lieutenant. He turned to leave.

"Hold on, Sergeant."

"Yes Sir." The sergeant turned back to the major's desk and leaned against the doorway.

"So, Habersham, how was your trip?" Major Dunney asked not really caring what the answer would be.

"A little bumpy Sir." The lieutenant immediately regretted the complaint, realizing that it sounded stupid.

"Well Lieutenant, you'll have plenty of time to heal up later. Tonight, I'm putting you on duty. Sergeant." The major held his hand out to the sergeant who handed the duty roster back. The major scribbled the lieutenant's name on it and gave it back to Sgt. Flint.

Sgt. Flint hardly looked like his name was a good fit. He was slight of build, bookish with dark rimmed glasses.

"Sergeant take the Lieutenant here and give him a quick tour then take him to the spotter's bunker."

"Yes Sir."

"Are you hungry Habersham?"

"Sir, I haven't eaten since breakfast and I guess I'm hungry."

"Sergeant, see the Lieutenant gets some dinner. Send it to the spotter's bunker." The major looked at Habersham and his overly starched uniform. "That good for you Lieutenant?"

"Yes Sir, thank you Sir." The lieutenant mentally cringed at the way his response drew a look of disgust from the major.

"Go!" The major waved his hand toward Sgt. Flint while looking at Lt. Habersham who jumped to his feet and snapped a salute. The major returned a half-hearted salute, then leaned back in his chair and crossed his arms.

The lieutenant and sergeant stepped out of the office into the stark concrete hallway. Corporal Grant stood by the lieutenant's duffle as if he were protecting a bag of gold.

"Just put the Lieutenant's duffle on that cot over there and get back to work Corporal."

"Sure thing Sergeant!" Corporal Grant seemed more than eager to be rid of his charge. He plopped the bag unceremoniously on an empty cot and disappeared down the hallway at a trot.

"Is this where I'm to be billeted?" The lieutenant incredulously queried pointing at the cot and duffle.

"No Sir. After your duty ends in the morning, you'll be taken over to the officer's barracks at Salt Creek, not far from here."

"Oh. I see."

"Sir, there's a latrine over there, I suggest you change to fatigues and grab your field jacket." The sergeant gestured to a door labeled 'latrine.'

A few minutes later, the lieutenant emerged in fatigues and laid his over starched class A uniform on the cot.

"There's a mess there too so's you can have a nice breakfast, but I'm afraid the best you'll get this evening is a box lunch." The sergeant looked at the lieutenant for a reaction. "Guess a sandwich is better than cold rations though."

"That'll be fine. I'm not really that hungry after all the turns and bumps in that damn truck." The lieutenant squinted trying to see the end of the hallway.

At the end of the hallway they came to a pair of heavy metal doors that wouldn't have looked out of place in a bank. The sergeant struggled to open one of the doors, but the lieutenant offered no help. As the lieutenant stepped through he felt a blast of cool fresh salt air. When his eyes adjusted to the soft light of the turret, his face froze in an expression that could have meant he had just stumbled into Betty Grable in a bathing suit.

"Holy mother of God." His voice just barely audible.

"She a beauty ain't she?" The sergeant smiled at the lieutenant's reaction. "It's a sixteen-incher. Navy gun, just like on a battleship!"

"This is what I'm spotting for?"

"This'n and one just like it 500 feet that way." The sergeant pointed at the door to the hallway.

"What the hell does it shoot?"

"Ah, sixteen-inch one-ton shells like those." The sergeant pointed to a trolley loaded with impressively wicked looking projectiles. "Real beauties ain't they?"

"Must make a hell of a racket." The lieutenant carefully touched the railing around the gun mount as if he suspected it was electrified. "I can't see the water from here, how do I spot for this thing?"

"I'll take you there. It's a small bunker down the hill from here." The sergeant pointed to an opening near where the barrel of the massive gun seemed to disappear into the mist. "This way Sir."

They emerged from the gun emplacement and started down a muddy path. The mist hung in patches everywhere, and the sun was beginning to lower on the western horizon. Thorny plants adjacent to the trail snagged at the lieutenant's uniform.

"That's blackberry Sir," said Sgt. Flint. "It grows everywhere around here. Really tasty, in pies and stuff."

"Can't it be cut back a little more?" The lieutenant carefully disengaged the thorny bush from the sleeve of his field jacket.

"Oh, we do Sir, it just grows back in days."

"Sounds like you know the local flora."

"Yes Sir. I'm from the Olympic Peninsula, over near Lake Crescent. I'm lucky to serve at Camp Hayden."

"How much farther Sergeant?"

"Oh, about fifty yards or so."

The lieutenant nearly fell twice on the wet, slippery path while the sergeant had the surefooted ease of a mountain goat. Flint stopped and turned to face the lieutenant, then gestured to what seemed to be a clump of bushes. There was a small concrete stairway that was dimly lit by a red light coming from inside.

Entering the bunker, the lieutenant first noticed that the entire interior was bathed in a mixture of red light coming from several overhead bulbs on a ceiling so low he had to stoop to avoid hitting his head. Sunlight streamed in from a long twelve-inch-high opening facing the Strait of Juan De Fuca. There were two stools near the opening, one of which was occupied by a private who was intently scanning the water with a pair of binoculars. Sensing the presence of the two new bunker occupants, he turned and saw the lieutenant. Jumping to his feet, the private bumped his head on the low ceiling which caused him to drop the heavy binoculars. The strap around his neck holding the binoculars yanked his head down and the binoculars banged into his chest.

"At ease Private." The gesticulation of the private struck the lieutenant as hilarious. But he stifled his laugh. "Anything to report?"

"Nothing unusual Sir. Just fishing boats, some freighters and a tanker." Private Williams was a slightly pudgy fellow with ruddy complexion and round friendly face. "The fog comes and goes, so it's kind of hard to see sometimes, Sir."

"Get the Lieutenant familiar with the bunker, Williams." Sgt. Flint turned and disappeared as quickly as he had appeared in Major Dunney's office, causing the lieutenant to wonder is he wasn't an apparition.

"Here Sir." Private Williams handed the lieutenant a pair of standard issue binoculars. The lieutenant put the leather strap around his neck and, raising them to his eyes, adjusted the focus to suit his vision.

Lt. Habersham moved over to an artillery range finder mounted on a tripod which seemed to take more space in the bunker than anything else save the two metal stools. He peered through the eyepiece twisting knobs to move the azimuth target to degrees east and west, north and south in degrees.

"Comms?"

"Over here Sir." Williams pointed to an army green bag on the shelf along the back of the bunker.

The lieutenant flipped the bag open and pulled out a field phone that resembled a large walkie-talkie. He extended the antennae and pressed the talk key. "Lieutenant Habersham, comm check."

"Who?" A voice crackled in response.

"Lieutenant Habersham in the spotter's bunker requesting a comm check." The lieutenant was only slightly irritated at the response, given the fact that he had just arrived.

There was a long pause. "Yes Sir, I don't know who you are, but I'm reading you four by four."

"Who is this?"

"Radioman Evers, Sir."

"Thank you, Radioman Evers, I'll comm check again in one hour." The lieutenant placed the field phone back in the bag and turned to Private Williams. "I hope they bring us chow soon, suddenly I'm starved."

"Should be here in about an hour Sir. There's some coffee on the shelf back there, might still be hot." Private Williams pointed to a small enameled pot sitting on a hot plate. There were several olive drab tin cups, one of which had a spoon, and was filled with sugar.

"Thanks, coffee sounds good." The lieutenant moved to the shelf and grabbed an empty cup, blowing in it as a reflex. He poured some of the black liquid, which smelled surprisingly wonderful. Steam rose from the cup in the cool air.

Coffee had become more available and of higher quality since the war in Europe had ended. The lieutenant sipped the hot liquid with the same reverence one might sip a single malt scotch. "Damn, that's really good!"

"Yes Sir. Chow's getting better too."

"Where you from Williams?" The lieutenant thought he'd get better acquainted with the fellow he was stuck with in this tight little dungeon.

"Phoenix, Arizona Sir."

"Pretty much the opposite of this huh? Miss the desert?"

"Sometimes, but it's nice here. Very quiet, Sir." The private continued to scan the water below.

"Seen any action Williams?"

"No Sir, just one stateside coastal battery after another."

"Yeah, that's my story too. Although this is my first assignment since artillery school." The lieutenant looked thoughtfully into his coffee cup. "I wanted the Pacific and I got it. Just the wrong side of the damn thing!"

After an hour, a private arrived with two small cardboard boxes from the mess hall. Private Williams took the boxes, thanking the mess private and handed one of the boxes to the lieutenant. To the lieutenant's surprise inside the box was an inviting looking turkey sandwich on brown bread wrapped in wax paper. A separate wax paper held lettuce, tomato and a slice of processed cheese so the recipient could add what they wished to the sandwich. There was a shiny red apple and a dark green packet labeled "cookies."

"This doesn't look too bad, actually."

"Oh no Sir, the chow here is good." Williams assembled his sandwich and took a bite. "Breakfast is really good!"

"I'll keep watch Private, go ahead and eat." The lieutenant raised his binoculars and began to search the Strait.

Patches of fog drifted across the water making it difficult to see clearly. The lieutenant couldn't see a single boat or ship, nor across the Strait to the Canadian shore which was usually visible on a clear day. In addition, the sun had begun to race toward the horizon, softening the available light.

"What the hell? Private do we have any subs coming through?" The lieutenant jumped to his feet.

The private grabbed a clipboard and fumbled through the papers attached to it. "No Sir, just a destroyer, but it went through hours ago."

"Shit! Shit! Williams look over there!" The lieutenant excitedly pointed to the west.

The private scanned the fog and water but didn't see anything. "What am I looking for Sir?"

"A sub I think! Dammit! I lost it. Right at the water line, between the water line and the fog." The lieutenant was frustrated now. "Crap! It was gray and rounded, it had to be a sub!"

"Holy crap Sir!" The private nervously scanned the water but still couldn't see anything. "How fast was it moving?"

"I don't know, not too fast." He strained to find the sub again. "Wait! There it is again!"

Williams scanned in the direction that the lieutenant was but still could not see what the lieutenant was talking about. "Sorry Sir, I can't see anything."

"There it is again, closer this time!" The lieutenant excitedly pointed at the water. He dropped the binoculars to his chest where they dangled on the leather strap and moved quickly to the range finder. "You see it yet Williams?"

The private adjusted his binoculars trying to verify the siting for the excited officer. He spotted a ripple in the water. "I think I see something."

"Give me the phone!" The lieutenant reached out his hand without taking his eyes from the range finder.

"You sure Sir?"

"Dammit our job is to spot the enemy, now give me the damn phone!" The lieutenant snapped the phone out of the private's hand and keyed the mic. "Comms, comms this is Lt. Habersham in the spotting bunker, come in!"

"Who?"

"Dammit Evers, it's Lt. Habersham. Get me the duty officer, NOW!" By this time the lieutenant was screaming into the phone. He quickly raised his binoculars trying to get a fix on his quarry. He again saw the hulking gray cylindrical object breaking the surface.

"This is Captain Collins, who is this?"

"Sir, this is Lt. Habersham in the spotting bunker. I've got what looks like a sub in the water sir. There's no Navy sub on the list sir!"

The captain turned to his sergeant. "Check with the Navy, see if they have a sub coming through the Strait."

The sergeant picked up the phone and contacted the Navy base at Bangor, Washington. After a short conversation, he turned and said in a 'matter of fact' tone, "No sir, they've got nothing in the Strait."

"Shit." The captain thought for a minute. "What do you see lieutenant?"

"It looks like one of those Jap minisubs, sir! Looks about forty or fifty feet and matches what I read about. We were briefed on these at Ventura Sir."

"Can you see any markings, or a conning tower?"

"Sir the Kaiten don't have any markings or a conning tower. They're suicide subs sir! Manned torpedoes!"

"Get a fix on it lieutenant, I'll get right back to you. Sergeant, get Major Dunney on the phone, now!"

"Yes sir!"

Things were rapidly getting exciting at Battery 131. The captain went to a metal box on the wall of the comm room and, pulling open the cover, turned a switch which set off a claxon horn. Down the concrete corridors solders were scrambling from their bunks and pulling on boots and shirts. Soon there was the sound shouting voices and boots on the concrete floors.

"Sir I have the major on the phone."

"What the hell is going on captain?" Major Dunney had been enjoying a nice plate of clams and mussels when he was summoned to the phone.

"Sir, the spotter has sighted a Kaiten in the Strait, you know, one of those Jap suicide subs."

"The hell you say!" The major narrowed his eyes. "Was it that new Lieutenant?"

"Habersham, yes Sir! But he seemed pretty sure about what he saw Sir."

The major was troubled by the lieutenant's short tenure at Battery 131. But he had been at Schofield Barracks, Pearl Harbor when the Japanese attacked in 1941. He heard about the Jap mini-subs used there. The Japanese were losing the war, and desperate attacks on Washington bases just might be something they would try. He couldn't take the chance. He wasn't going to hesitate like they did at Pearl.

"Did you check with the Navy?"

"Yes Sir. They've got nothing in the water."

"Then blow the damn thing the hell out of the water!" Major Dunney hung up the phone. "Damn."

Gunners scrambled to load the massive shells and bags of powder into guns #1 and #2. Blind to the target, the gunners relied on coordinates from the spotter. Adrenaline pulsed through every soldier in Battery 131. The guns had never been fired, even in practice. There had been no indication that this was a drill.

"Evers, get me that lieutenant in the spotting bunker, and I need comms to the guns!"

"Yes Sir!" Radioman Evers was now as sharp as a knife edge. "Ready Sir."

"Habersham! I need coordinates on the target, now!"

"Yes, Sir!" Lt. Habersham had been tracking the hulking gray object. He peered through the range finder. He had a good view of the target sliding through the water. It would be necessary for the lieutenant to calculate the speed and position of the target, and where it would be when the giant guns could swing into action.

"Sir, guns to 25 degrees north, 30 degrees east. Advise when ready."

Captain Collins picked up the microphone that was connected to the gun crews.

"Guns one and two, 25 degrees north, 30 degrees east. Advise when ready."

There was a short pause as the gun crews cranked the big guns into position.

"Gun one ready Sir!"

"Gun two ready Sir!"

"Spotter, status!"

"Target steady Sir, will advise when in range."

"Gunners, ready on my signal." The captain felt his chest tighten.

Lieutenant Habersham carefully tracked the target. His heart was pounding. He finally was in the war.

"On my mark, three, two, one FIRE!"

"Gun one, fire, gun two fire." The captain's order resulted in an explosion of gun fire that none of those at Battery 131 had ever heard. The ground shook and the shockwave seemed to suck the breath out everyone manning the guns.

Lt. Habersham could not see the enormous flame that emitted from each gun, but the flash illuminated everything around the bunker, and it shook so hard it nearly knocked the lieutenant and private off their feet. They both grabbed their binoculars and rushed to the observation slot.

There erupted two huge plumes of water in the Strait. The lieutenant and private both strained to observe if the target had been hit and sunk.

"Look! There! You see it Williams?" The lieutenant saw chunks of debris in the water.

"I see it Sir! Wreckage everywhere! You did it Sir, you did it!" The private almost hugged the lieutenant but held back despite his excitement.

"Spotter report!" The captain was anxious, and his voice reflected it.

"Sir, target destroyed! Debris in the water. No more movement observed."

Next morning, at the Camp Hayden officer's mess, Major Dunney patted Lt. Habersham on the shoulder as the lieutenant enjoyed a breakfast of pancakes, bacon and coffee. "Good work lieutenant."

"Thank you, sir." The lieutenant was enjoying all the accolades from the officers and gun crews.

"We've asked the Coast Guard to search the debris field. We should hear from them shortly." Major Dunney poured a cup of coffee for himself, then gave the lieutenant a 'warm up.'

After about an hour of talking and laughing, a Coast Guard lieutenant commander entered the mess and was greeted by the major.

"What did you find, Commander?"

"Well Major, let me show you." The commander motioned to two coast guardsmen who had come with him.

They walked over to the table where Lt. Habersham was sitting and placed something wrapped in canvas. They unwrapped the object to reveal a shiny gray slab with a gelatinous substance attached. It smelled fishy.

"Congratulations Major, you've sunk a California Gray whale!" The commander attempted to conceal his amusement.

"A whale? Not a Jap sub? Dammit Lieutenant you said it was a Kaiten!" The major was red in the face. He stormed out of the mess mumbling something about command was going to have his ass.

As soon as he was gone the entire room erupted into laughter, except of course Lt. Habersham who looked as if he'd just been told that Christmas was cancelled.

The commander patted the lieutenant on the shoulder. "Nothing to blubber over Lieutenant."

The room erupted in even louder laughter.

Captain Collins chipped in. "Well, we will all have whale of a 'tail' to tell our grandkids."

Lt. Habersham buried his head in hands. "I killed a whale? I love whales! I killed a whale!"

Three weeks later, Army Air Corps B-29s dropped incredibly powerful and horrifying bombs on the Japanese cities of Hiroshima and Nagasaki resulting in thousands of casualties. It was thought that these bombings saved millions of American and Japanese lives that an invasion would surely have claimed. The Japanese surrendered.

Battery 131 at Camp Hayden was decommissioned in 1948. The 16" guns were scrapped. Broken apart, they were sold for $30 per ton. They were never actually used against the enemy.

No records have been found of the sinking of a California Gray Whale by U.S. Army Coastal Gun Battery 131. Many duty records from World War II have long been lost or destroyed.

Author Intro

JOAN ENOCH, MD

I'm a psychiatrist/psychoanalyst who has lived all across this country. I was raised in N.Y. with stopovers in Illinois, North Carolina, and Mississippi during W.W.II, where I was spit at for being Jewish. I raised my two sons in Philadelphia, moved to Arizona for work in my fifties, Florida at sixty, and Oregon near seventy. I made it to the Olympic Peninsula at the tender age of seventy-six, having a son and his family in the vicinity.

I started writing poetry in my sixth decade when my second husband was diagnosed with a brain tumor. I have been a student of Buddhist philosophy and Consciousness studies for many years, published poems in Arizona publications and a chapbook called *Shiva Dancing*, and facilitated classes, many about writing poetry for healing and just for the joy of writing.

I love the game of poker and play in my spare time. To me it resembles the game of life. Can one win or lose with equal aplomb? Not easy to do but one can try.

Joan can be reached at justbojo@yahoo.com for consultation on poetry, healing, or just to say hello.

LET IT BE HERE

If my life must wind down, as lives must,
Let it be here
Where glaciated mountains meet the sea.
Between them towns dress diffidently
Differently, curtsying to the elements.

Purple haze of lavender, white sails seen
Near spits that caress the strait and bays.
Ferries ply back and forth to islands
Sparkling in sunlight, drenching us in
Mist and rain; Juan de Fuca holds court.

From my new home, a ribbon of water
Graces the green of grasses and trees
Everywhere birdsong, a doe and fawns
Graze, offset by honking geese settling,
Raising their growing goslings in safety.

If my life must lose energy, as lives must
Let it be here
In this Eden-like land, remotely removed
From the turmoil of a country
At war with itself.

Let me daydream here, on occasion
In the days that are left to me
That all is fair and just, and in this
Pastoral place let me pretend,
At least for a time
That all is well with the world.

THE ICE SHEET

Written after full moon talk in May, near Railroad Bridge

The ice sheet slowly formed, moving south
Covering much of the land of the peninsula.
Melting later, over the years
Leaving the land to thrive, the flora and fauna
Proliferating under the mighty Olympics.

Many eons pass, and an Ordinance island
With its high crane, sits there in
Port Townsend Bay. It fills, in the darkness
of night, more and more ships
With armaments, that can wreak havoc.

The Hood Canal Bridge opens
Spitting out Nuclear subs
Into the wider world.
Partying on the bridge; the regal sight
Causes excitement, photo ops, and horror.

The beaches team with SEALS
At sub-dawn, storming ashore;
The wrong kind of seals, mind you
While planes scream down the strait
Noise pollution, disturbing our Eden.

Will wars ever leave our earth island
Adrift in the silent, spectral void?
If we as a species must pass away,
Instead of humans killing humans,
I'd personally prefer the ice sheet!

Author Intro

DIANNE L. KNOX

Poetry is breathing. I have no choice.

My active life of Tai Chi, traveling, hiking, art-walking, dancing, reading, talking with friends are my passions. Life is my prompt.

My degree is from the University of Iowa. I live with my rescue, Kitanofugi (Kita), named after a Grand Sumo Champion, in my ideal home, Sequim.

I can be found reading my verses aloud most Fourth Fridays in Sequim, Third Tuesdays in Port Townsend at Better Living Through Coffee, First Thursday at The Keg and I in Chimicum, and Northwind Gallery for the Ekphrastic Writings. I am published in *Tidepools, In the Words of Olympic Peninsula Authors* 2017, and *Spontaneous Writing by Twenty Courageous Writers*. I am working on a memoir and hope to have a volume of my own poetry soon, entitled *Red Hot Pepper*.

You can contact Dianne at dianneknox@icloud.com or ddiseth@q.com.

AWAKENING

We met over salmon
Talked of wild rice
And tomatoes
Our appetites salivating the gamut

So intimate
I knew his experience
By his lines – facial, spoken, not
His white hair, not white lies

He almost reached for my hand
Or a soft touch of my wrist
I looked into his eyes briefly
Took in his un-ringed finger cautiously

I would grow tomatoes
In lots of sun, little wind
Not now, but next year, in spring
And, we would meet

Again to discuss
His wife's recipe for
Perfect pesca, baked tomatoes, rice
And I would drool over their relationship.

COPPER RIVER SALMON

Almost a year has passed
Since the Copper River run
Drew us to the cooler to discuss
Wild rice and tomatoes with this salmon

I will go back to our meeting space
Wait for him, hoping to recapture the awakening
I'm not obsessed with him
Think of him only occasionally

Remembering his advice on planting
Cultivating perfect weather for growth
Anticipating ingredients
Coming together

I would welcome a re-kindling
Firing up the grill
But, the tomatoes won't be ready yet
I am ready now.

FOGHORNS

The foghorns remind me of you
Their low humming voice haunting and soothing
Calling out that The Strait is not safe today
Best rest until all is clear

Fishing will be postponed or called off
You will linger near me
I will feel your breath resume its sleep
The fish will be safe, as I will
Bait will wait in the freezer
Rods, reels, hooks, line stowed
Prepared for another warmer day

The foghorns remind me of you
As calming as your voice protecting me from crashing
Calling out to me to avoid obstacles and harm
Halibut will sleep in their deep beds
Knowing your skillful casting won't reach them this day

The foghorns remind me of you
But, then, so does everything.

FRUIT

You would share your fruit with me
Unfolding that knife always on your hip
Symmetrically slice an apple wedge
Hand it to me on the blade, sharp toward you

You would peel orange skin
Tear sections, offer me juicy parts
Satisfy my appetites
With your generous quenching

Like your knowledge on subjects new to me
Flipping open a world to savor
Flavored slices of life
Relishing each piece of our time together

You would share your life with me
Handing me pleasurable moments
Protecting me with your blade
Sharp side toward harm – any kind.

KEEN'S RED HOT PEPPER

Dream girl
Lost in the count
Concentrating so completely
Not to trip over the line

Her red hot energy
Disturbing the status quo
Shaking and shaping her future
With each swing and jump

Stay within the boundaries
Don't get caught outside
The protective whirling air
Secure in the rope zone

Lives spent
Jumping over obstacles
While presenting
A tranquil, soothing image

Confident behavior be-getting
Confident behavior
Helping her not trip and stumble
Out of control on life's steps and missteps.

MONDAY MORNING

Wash day, Monday
Here, a woman's clothesline
A woman's clothes align
Neatly on a line, today, Monday
Looks like life on the line

Living alone loving alone
Washing alone hanging alone
Dreaming alone
Almost over mourning
Now, Monday morning
Looks like love on the line

Her white, pure clothes hanging
Hanging dreams on the line
Dreams hanging on the line
Dreams washed in living life
Looks like dreams on the line

Her life exposed by sun
Her lacy camisole hanging lovingly
Her lacy skirt danced the night away
Lacy jacket warmed her on her way
Cleansed by light
Fresh, revealed insight
Looks like myself on the line

Just enough sun today, Monday
Just enough clouds to dry, mid-day
Just enough green to be serene
Just enough orange poppies to be seen

How fragile these poles
Caving, bending like a vine
Under cotton weight waiting to dry in time
Before clouds burst the healing
Waiting for Tuesday to relieve the line

Scrubbed clean, hanging, exposed, dried
Looks like life on the line.

OUTAGE

I smell light
Though not you
Who dwarfs the spectrum
Waxing memories

True flickering tales
Of fires catching my breath
Exhaling flames
Inextinguishable thoughts

I smell light
Wicks of warmth
Spreading glow
Onto this night

I smell light
Inhaling heat
From our embers
That will never go out.

QUICKSAND

He was my quicksand
Once my toe was tipped
There was no removal
Sinking into him
No way back

No wanting to go back
Once I realized I couldn't

Sinking slowly
Each inch of disappearing flesh
Swallowed by his smile, his face
Pulling me deeper, inescapable

Time was short
Or was it long
It passed
As I passed under
The spell
The pull

He was my quicksand.

ROSE

This live Rose is not as exquisite
As the plastic-stemmed
Polyester-petaled one you gave me years ago
When price was an object
Cost cannot compete with feeling
Overwhelming love spreading open
Each day it survives
Permanent in expression

No drooping head
Falling crinkled leaves

A Rose is not a Rose
Unless it has been
Named in passion
Appreciated by thought
Given in sincerity
Lasting a memory's length.

SPIRIT

Another spirit has left my home
Proving again that there is
No limit to the number of tears
Or amount of love

Available in one body
Mine.

A furry spirit is like
A fleshy spirit
In its expanse
Its reward
Its ability to
Vibrate me
Shake my emotions
Shape my response

Cause tears to well and spill
Cause love to swell and ache
There is nothing that can
Halve the tears
Nothing can cap the love
They fertilize and feed each-other
Growing unending emotional floods
Incalculable love.

TO YOUR HEALTH

What would you say if I told you
If you shake Cumin on your Avocado
The two synergize to prevent Alzheimer's

That pepper-caused sneezing
Empties your senses of toxins.
Without that lettuce, even iceberg,
Your colon would untwist
Turn your gut inside out

If you combine mushrooms,
Red onion, red pepper, cucumber
The sugar in your salad dressing
Is canceled.

What would you say if the best if used-by date
Makes this jar taste better after that date
If I refrigerate before opening
The contents are overly-preserved

We try to eat properly
Fork on the left, knife right
But, what we cut and stab
What we pick at or savor

Changes its value
By the foods' champions,
Promoters, book sales, studies
All beyond the foods' caloric, nutritional
Organic, synthetic make-up

Confusing, contradictory
Voices on our choices
At the cost of our health
Longing to feed our starving souls

WHAT IF WE DISCOVER

What if we discover one day
That broccoli has feelings
Cries like a Lobster immersed
In boiling water
Stares at you with green eyes
Sneezes when garnished

What if we discover one day
That a perfected Ancestry.com
Finds everything is related
Down to our atoms
Not just Adams Apples
DNA don't lie

What if we discover one day
That sand and grass scream
When you step or make castles
Rocks long for your warm touch
In trade for minerals
Trees are really waving at you
Sun exchanges its heat with yours

Our mutual water make up
Pulls us together with the tide
Joining us with clouds
Life our common goal
Double helix exchanging
Breath with greenery
Carbon Dioxide for Oxygen
Co-existing with the wind

What if we discover one day
That our only verbal connection
Is through a poem
Speaking all tongues
In one shared note, a vibration
Touching all of our senses
Uniting our reasons for being

What if we discover today
That we are infants in our understanding.

Author Intro

MARY ANN MILLER

I am a wife, a mother and a grandmother. Those are the most important things in my life. I live in Port Angeles with my husband of thirty-three years. I spent my childhood in California, but I love living in the Pacific Northwest, and now I cannot imagine living anywhere else. Once my family was grown, and I retired from a career in accounting, I found myself wanting to use the other side of my brain. I started writing.

I am inspired by my family, encouraged by my writing friends and grateful for the wealth of writing opportunities on the Olympic Peninsula. I write memoir, short story and occasionally I write nonfiction. I am currently working on my first novel.

I have been published in Peninsula College's literary magazine *Tidepools*, *Sew Beautiful* magazine, *Stamper's Sampler*, and had a short story presented in a local readers' theater production.

Mary Ann can be reached at Millermaryann0@gmail.com.

THE PYSHT TRAIL

It had been a long and tiring trip, but Ellen could barely restrain her excitement. She sat in front of the fire in the lodging house and wrote what would be the last letter on her journey.

December 15, 1891
Dear Mother,
We took the Steamer Hermosa from Port Angeles to Pysht yesterday. It was a three-hour trip. When we arrived at Pysht we had to wait on board in a heavy swell, until a small boat came alongside to take us and our luggage ashore. The weather was unsettled all the way and poor Nels got sick. It upset him that he got sick, when no one else did.

Pysht is on the coast, west of Port Angeles. Today we will continue on foot, twenty miles to Beaver. Some of the trail guides will continue south from Beaver to Forks. That is eleven miles farther than I will have to walk.

I am so glad that I did not have to make this journey alone. Peter's sister, Anna, has been a godsend. And I have already fallen in love with young Nels and little Hannah. Anna's husband, Oscar, is a bit gruff and impatient with the children, but I think he is afraid of the unknowns ahead.

I changed from my traveling suit to my walking skirt this morning. It is muddy and wet here so I am sure the shorter skirt will be better for today's trek to Beaver. I just hope that my bloomers don't peek out from beneath it.

Oscar says that today's walk will be the toughest part of our trip so I am anticipating a long and tiring day. But if it all looks like Pysht, it will be beautiful. Washington is very different than Kansas.

It is hard for me to believe that I will see Peter before today is over, and by tomorrow night I will be his wife.

Anna has just called to me, so I must close and post this so that we can join the other settlers that are following the pack train today.

Your loving daughter,

Ellen

Ellen hurried to the desk, pulled two coins from her pocket and paid the postage for her letter home. Then she followed Anna out of the lodging house to join the others. She was barely through the door when she heard Oscar yell, "Hurry up Nelson. We don't want to be left behind."

Ellen feared that she might have been the reason for Oscar's frustration. She hurried up to the eleven-year-old and squeezed his shoulder. Nels looked up at Ellen and then, hiding his tears, he looked quickly away. She gave him a quick hug before she nudged him along.

There were six settlers returning to their homesteads in Beaver and Bear Creek. By the time Anna and Ellen joined the group everyone seemed to know that Peter's bride and sister were traveling with them. A gruff looking homesteader held out his hand to Ellen and said, "I'm Charley. I promised Peter I would make sure you arrived safely. If you need anything just let me know."

Ellen tried to hide her smile as she shook his hand.

A light snow fell and a slight breeze made the air seem even colder than it was. Ellen buttoned her coat to her neck and tied a hat on her head. She couldn't help but notice that all of the settlers wore wool caps. She wished she had one too.

Just beyond Pysht they crossed the river on a log. Grouse and rabbits scampered along the brush. Hannah tried to chase them. Several times Oscar's voice echoed through the trees, "Hannah, keep moving. There is no time to play today."

A couple of miles farther it was necessary to cross the river again. This crossing was much wider than the first one. The bridge was another log. This one was worn smooth by previous travelers and was icing up from the cooling temperatures. While the pack horses entered the water to cross, Charley caught up with Ellen. "Miss Ellen, you'll need this." He handed her a long branch. "It's a walking stick," he responded to her puzzled look. "Put it into the water as you cross. It will help you keep your balance." Then he hurried over the log and waited.

Little Hannah followed Charley across the log in front of her soon-to-be aunt. She was nearly half-way across when her feet went out from under her. Without thinking about her own safety, Ellen reached forward and caught the child just before she slid into the river. If it had not been for the walking stick, they both would have ended up in the freezing water. When Charley heard the two females gasp he took two big steps back onto the log, picked up the little girl, and carried her across. Then he reached out to Ellen to help her off the log.

Safely on the other side, she stood and shivered . . . not from cold, but from fear. She hugged Hannah and tried to hide her own distress as she dried the child's tears with her gloved hand.

For the next several miles they hiked through a valley of thick timber. Ellen could not identify the trees; they bore little resemblance to the box elder and sycamores she knew from Kansas. From time to time Charley would say, "This is a hemlock," or "This is a spruce." She tried to think of something to associate with each species so that she would be able to identify it later.

Deer tracks crossed the trail, but the travelers never saw the animals. The Pysht River was always near. When they reached Burnt Mountain, Charley identified it too. They left the river at the mountain and began to cross the divide. Snow swirled around them and grew deeper.

"How much farther?" cried Hannah. Everyone ignored her question. Charley finally picked the small child up and placed her on his shoulders.

Ellen too, wondered how much farther but she did not ask. She stomped her feet trying to loosen the snow that had caked on her boots. Each step was agony. She stuck her hands into her coat pockets trying to keep them warm. It was impossible now to keep them dry.

Without warning, the divide lowered them into another valley. The sun came out. The ground was nearly dry. It was as if they had been transported into a different land. The pack train stopped to rest the horses. Anna handed Ellen and the children a snack of hardtack and jerky. "Do you think we are over the worst part of the trail?" Anna asked.

When they started moving again Oscar insisted that the children travel between he and Anna. Ellen was in front of them as they started to climb another mountain. The trail was steep. Again snow packed the way. Wind howled. Snow-covered branches had to be pushed out of the way for them to stay on the path. The snow was wet and heavy. It filtered into their boots. Ellen's wet feet scared her. She knew about frostbite, but had never experienced it. She heard the children cry out, but she did not look back. Instead she focused on the trail ahead and put one foot in front of the other. She thought about Peter. It had been nearly a year since he had left Kansas. Over and over she reminded herself that she would see him again tonight.

They climbed for several miles. The trail narrowed. To their right was a deep crevice filled with giant trees but no visible bottom. The ledge narrowed until all that they could do was put one foot directly in front of the other.

Suddenly a loud roar pierced the air as snow and rock charged down into the gap below. Ellen could see the landslide barreling down the side of the trail, but she could not see what was around the bend. She held her breath. For several minutes no one moved or said a word.

Charley turned and said. "Stay put. Stay as close to the mountain as you can. Do not move until I get back." And then he disappeared around the bend.

All manner of fear went through Ellen's mind. Did someone go down with the slide? Was the trail blocked? Would they have to turn around and go back? If the trail was blocked when would she see Peter? It seemed as if they waited forever.

When Charley finally returned he said, "We'll be moving again soon."

"What happened? Is everyone okay?" she asked.

"It's okay. Something spooked one of the mail horses and he went over the edge."

Eyes wide, Ellen stared at him. "Did they save the horse?"

Charley looked toward the children and shook his head. "We'll be moving along soon," he repeated. "Just stay as close to the ledge as you can."

When they started forward Ellen was afraid to raise her eyes above the trail. It was narrow and rocky, and covered in ice. She tentatively placed one foot in front of the other, testing the ground with each step. *Take us safely across,* she prayed, knowing that one misstep could send them spiraling into the gulch below.

Eventually they began to descend the other side of the mountain. Just when Ellen thought she couldn't take another step, the trail improved and soon there was increased chatter among the settlers.

What had been miles of silence and fear soon turned to joy as they spotted Fifteen-Mile-House in the distance. Mr. Welsh was waiting for them when they arrived at his ranch on Beaver Lake. The weary travelers gathered inside to rest and warm up.

Ellen and the children crowded together near the fire to warm their hands and feet, while Mr. Welsh scurried around preparing a dinner of mountain trout. Charley approached her and said, "Only five more miles." Then he moved on to talk with the other settlers. Ellen wasn't sure if she should be encouraged that they had already covered fifteen of the twenty miles, or discouraged that she had five more miles to go.

Warmed and fed, the settlers gathered outside. Now that she was warmed Ellen could see how beautiful the lake was. She tried to paste a picture of it in her mind so that she could describe it in her next letter home.

The horses started to move, and the settlers followed. The rumbling of a waterfall pierced through the winter quiet. They could not see it from the trail, but Charley assured Ellen that it was a sign that they were getting close.

Not far past the falls, the settlers and pack horses split into two groups. Anna, Oscar and the children followed the group heading east to Bear Creek where they would be homesteading. Ellen remained with Charley and the group heading west to Beaver. This was the first time she had been without Anna and Oscar.

It started to snow again and the wind whistled through the trees. The sun had set by the time they dropped down into the Beaver Prairie where there were only two visible structures. Both were rugged and weathered. To Ellen neither building looked sturdy enough to stand the winter wind. Charley pointed to a two-story structure and said, "That's the hotel." Then he pointed at another smaller building that was little more than a shack and said, "That's the storeroom. Peter is probably in the hotel."

Ellen was relieved to have survived the trail, but tears filled her eyes as she said to the afternoon wind, "Oh Peter, what have you gotten us into?"

Author Intro

JUDITH A. LINDBERG

I write poetry for any reason or any season. I am a retired school counselor for the Port Angeles School District. My writing focus is poetry and prose. My poetry has been published in twelve of June Cotner's anthologies. I have had several poems published in a variety of magazines, and I have been a freelance writer for our local newspaper, the *Peninsula Daily News*. I am the author of one published book, *Moonbeams and Mud Puddles*. I am also a qualified proofreader for any needs, including court transcripts.

You can reach Judith at judilindberg@gmail.com.

IN STILLNESS

To see the grandeur of majestic mountains,
Snow-capped sentries, carved on a cobalt sky.
To hear the fragile flutter of whirling wings,
Hovered hummingbird in a serene summer garden.

Visions of vibrancy and bold vividness,
Sounds of nature's gentle, wondrous children,
To lift the spirit, to soothe the soul,
For now, this moment . . . peaceful,
In stillness.

PERSPECTIVES

I want to go back,
To the Sunday drives with Mom and Dad and the promise
   of Dairy Queen at the end,
The cones of soft vanilla swirl, topped by the chocolate or
   lime green magic shell,
That always dripped down my chin, no matter how many
   napkins I used.
I want to leave reality road just for a while.

I want to go back,
To when my dad wore striped overalls and a white shirt, with
   rolled-up sleeves,
And drove a Langendorf bread truck, with his name painted
   boldly on the driver's door.
He'd stop for coffee with Mom, sit on the kitchen stool, and they
   talked about their day.
He let me dance, in my stocking feet, right on top of his black
   work shoes.

I want to go back,
To sit on the cement step, by the back door, with my mom,
I'd munch on peanut butter and honey sandwiches
And sip on Nesbitt's orange or strawberry pop on those hot
   summer days.
Mom and I would watch tiny black ants, scurrying past our feet,
With cargoes of bread crumbs, the load slowing their journey,
But not their determination.

I want to go back,
To my red bike, the one with metallic sheen, the bike that I'd
   wanted for so long,

The bike with the handlebar tassels, the silver bell, the headlight,
And the black and white saddlebags, vinyl, of course.
I would ride proudly to the nearby store, on summer days,
And bring back ice cream bars for me and Mom.

I want to go back,
To comic book trading, bike hikes, daydreaming, imagining cloud
    shape possibilities,
Reading, hour by hour, unconcerned with the passing of time,
When "just being" was an entire world of contentment.
I want to go back,
To when Mom and I walked downtown to shop,
And then visited my grandmother, on the way home, to show off
    our new clothes,
To when Mom and I played Scrabble at the dining room table.
She was so patient and taught me the love of words.

I want to go back,
To when Dad and I drove to the Spit to watch the fishing boats
    come in
And where we skipped rocks across straits – Dad was skillful,
    I was not,
Standing on the beach that actually existed then, with sand and
    driftwood treasures,
To when we stopped at Woody's Coffee Shop for doughnuts,
    when Dad played dice,
And for the huge chocolate doughnuts with thick, fudge icing,
    free if Dad won!

I want to go back, now, today, this minute.
I want to go back because it's too difficult, here, in the real world.
Sometimes I feel like the ant, but not as determined.
I know I can't go back, but it is my own place to visit,
My memories of gold, my sweet journey of nostalgia.

Author Intro

CHARLIE SHELDON

I have been a commercial fisherman, a merchant sailor, and worked for ports on both coasts for thirty years. My knowledge of the sea and the Olympic Peninsula get together in my newest novel, *Adrift*. Here's a bit of the plot:

The *Seattle Express*, a 700-foot container ship bound for Seattle, is on fire in the Gulf of Alaska. Three hundred miles away, on the Olympic Peninsula, Larry and Louise fire up their old tug, *Warhorse*, and head into the open ocean to salvage the burning vessel. It's a race against time, the elements, and other high-speed tugs hot on *Warhorse's* tail.

This book is an exciting sequel to *Strong Heart*. Where that story took readers deep into the wilderness of the Pacific Northwest, *Adrift* carries it into a beautiful, brutal frontier of ice, wind, slicing cold, roiling waves, and ancient, mystic faith.

Adrift will be available in local book stores and online in autumn of 2018.

ADRIFT

Chapter One
December 5, Steve

The fire klaxon in my cabin howled. I jerked awake, sat up, and grabbed my clothing. I headed for the bridge one deck above, holding the handrails, staggering up the stairs, the ship shuddering into a rising sea, rolling. When the klaxon sounded I had been having my nightmare. The nightmare always came when the weather was really rough. This December, the Gulf of Alaska, the wind blowing seventy, eighty miles an hour, it was rough.

Wisps of smoke drifted in the dim wheelhouse, catching my throat. The klaxon chattered and Anne, my third mate, stood transfixed, her hand hovering over the general alarm. Wind whistled over the wheelhouse. Rain rattled against the windows. Water slid across the dark glass, beyond which I saw faint, dark containers, spray, huge seas rising. The alarm panel against the aft bulkhead was blinking like a Christmas tree.

"Shut that thing off," I said, meaning the klaxon. I understood why Anne hadn't sounded the general alarm. All the alarm panels were blinking, an obvious short. The klaxon had been tripping since we'd left Petropavlovsk a week earlier, becoming so irritating to those on watch they'd even placed a wooden matchstick beneath the toggle to keep the alarm silent. Of course when I saw what they'd done, I'd removed it. This smoke was real. There was a fire somewhere.

Now the bilge alarm went off.

I held on as the ship rolled. William was at the helm. I never understood how someone as tall and heavy as William could stand like a cat when the ship rolled. He stood by the wheel, looking ahead, his enormous frame braced, his wandering eye facing me. I peered at the alarm panel and jammed one of the toggles. "Check below, Anne. William, check the panels up here."

Anne ran below to check the cabin decks, one by one. It was the hour before dawn. The black night was thick with blowing rain and snow. I studied the panel. All the lights were flashing. The bilge alarm kept ringing. A huge sea boarded, filling the deck on the starboard side, foaming between the containers. I peered at the bilge display below the alarm panel. High water in number two hold forward. Wasn't that the sensor we'd replaced in Dutch Harbor a trip ago? Hadn't the first engineer checked it just last night? He'd gone forward after dinner, muttering something about the hold and the sensors.

Was the smoke thicker?

William opened panels beneath the console and indicators, one by one, checking for smoke and fire. He was on his hands and knees. The phone rang from the engine room.

"Smoke in the port tunnel, captain." Carlton, nearly as old as me, the third engineer, on watch below, was matter-of-fact. "Lots of smoke."

Anne emerged from climbing the stairs, out of breath, shaking her head. I sounded the general fire alarm. The big horn blasted, steady, for more than ten seconds.

"I have her," I said, holding the phone. "Get below."

Anne and William went below to join the rest of the crew at the fire station by the engine control center on the main deck. If there was smoke in the wheelhouse where I stood, and smoke in the tunnel along the port side below the main deck, whatever was happening was serious.

"The whole alarm panel fired off up here, Carlton. Seems like a short, but there's smoke up here. How is it in the tunnel?"

"Thick smoke, Captain. The Chief's gone forward, in his fire suit, tanks, taking a look."

"Let me know what you find, Carlton." I spoke quietly, forcing myself to remain calm. Last thing anyone needed right now was the captain screaming, and I was known to sometimes scream.

Here we were, just before dawn, terrible weather and the ship miles from land, smoke high and low. We had no idea where the fire was, or what kind of fire we had. The next few minutes were critical.

"You say, in the tunnel?" I asked. "Not in the engine room?"

An engine room fire is a sailor's worst nightmare. Another sea boarded. We'd slowed the ship at dusk the evening before, bringing her down to 42 revolutions - 10 knots - and still she was pounding and shuddering. Fighting a fire in this weather, wherever the fire was, would be almost impossible. Ahead, in the dark, rain drove against the deckhouse. Spray swept in huge swaths across the stacked containers. I could barely see forward.

"In the port tunnel, Steve." Carlton spoke calmly. He was old school. We'd come up nearly together. "Some of the lube oil canisters in the tunnel are on fire. Butch is reporting fire in the clarifier room."

The clarifier room was in the engine room, forward, next to the tunnel with smoke, port side. What happened to the sensors down there?

"Fire team in place, hoses rigged." Randall, my young first mate and designated fire captain, sounded steady on the phone. I heard other people, speaking beyond Randall, and they sounded steady, too. For a moment, I felt pride: my guys were calm, here. They needed to be calm.

Ahead, through the rain, I saw flames. As the ship plowed forward, the wind whipped the flames higher, rising before stacked containers. Now, against the flame, I saw thick smoke. How long had the fire been burning up there? How long had we been steaming into the wind, fanning the flames?

I've seen three ship fires in the forty years I've been sailing, two in the engine room. All were put out in minutes. All were terrifying. Now, on a ship longer in the teeth of her life than I was in the teeth of mine, a ship cobbled together with jury-rigs, old sensors, and air valves needing to be exercised but still often jammed shut, I was facing a fire I was sure had been burning for hours forward without anyone knowing, without any sensors firing.

Randall spoke clearly and loudly:

"Team One in place, Captain. The Chief went into the tunnel. The tunnel's bad. Our engine room guys cannot get into their suits because they're stored on the port side in the tunnel and the smoke's too bad. The wiper says there's flames coming out the clarifier room door. Team One has hoses and will try to get the clarifier fire. I have two guys in the starboard tunnel seeing what's hot over there. They haven't reported back yet."

Randall was thirty-four, the same age as my son Jimmie, who I'd been dreaming about when the klaxon went off. Randall was exactly the high performing youngster-in-a-hurry I'd dreamed Jimmie might be, years ago. This trip I'd been hard on Randall because he suffered no lack of self-esteem, and unless he developed some depth he would never be the kind of officer he believed he already was. Randall thought he knew everything. Luckily, in the area of fire control and emergency management, he damned near did know everything. Looking at the flames forward, I knew knowing everything in this case might not be enough.

"Randall be careful," I said. "I'm turning the ship, to get her running before the wind so the wind won't fan the flames further. Tell your guys to hang on."

I shifted to hand steering, took the wheel, and began turning to starboard. The ship rolled forty degrees as we came crosswise to the big seas. Water poured over the deck. As we turned, I saw the flames ahead, whipping away to starboard. It took time to turn. While we turned my nightmare came before me. I was standing under a pewter sky before eleven-year-old Jimmie, almost a quarter century ago, shortly after my happy, gleeful son, who once drank my words like truth, suffered his accident, becoming distant, remote. Jimmie's small frame, bulky in autumn clothing, slouched in the wheelchair next to the playground merry-go-round, head lowered, silent. My perfect little boy, there but lost. I wanted to place an arm around those small shoulders and gather him close, safe, and warm. I wanted to fill him with promise and hope. But I was frozen, unable to move, unable to speak, just there, helpless, as the future roared towards us. I struggled to speak, reach for Jimmie, offer him comfort from the dark days ahead, but what comfort could I offer? What comfort had I ever offered?

I turned the ship until the wind was coming at the stern. Big following seas now overtook us. The wind was blowing at least seventy knots. The flames and smoke sped away, forward, cloaking the forward mast and the bow. There was a lot of flame and smoke.

First we had to get the clarifier room fire out, then the tunnel fire, and then the fire in the hold up forward. Even running before the wind, we couldn't go on deck – we were still taking heavy water over the rail.

Randall's voice shook.

"Starboard tunnel has smoke, too, captain. Port tunnel fire worse; now the fluids are burning. The fire in the clarifier room is spreading and my guys can't work down there more than ten minutes before sucking their tanks dry. It's bad, Captain."

None of the engine room crew could help with the fire because their suits and tanks had been stored in the burning tunnel. This left only fire team Number One and already they were using reserve air tanks. Randall took a deep breath. I could hear him despite all the background noise, and I knew what he was going to say even as he spoke.

"I recommend, captain, we abandon the engine room and try the Halon."

The engine room space was configured so we could isolate the space, then flood the area with Halon gas. Halon pushes the oxygen out of an enclosed space, which helps force a fire out. This meant everyone had to leave the engine room.

"We have guys burned already, captain."

"Do it," I said. If the Halon didn't work, it wouldn't be long before the fire rose into the deckhouse. The seas were enormous. The sky had brightened. The scene before me was grim. Huge rollers marched from behind, overtaking the ship. The wind whipped the wave crests. Flames forward flickered higher and higher. There was now heavy smoke in the wheelhouse, obviously coming up from below, creeping through the decks. The fire would be racing into the deckhouse in minutes.

Even if the Halon worked in the engine room, fire had spread throughout the ship, and when the generators shut down, as they eventually would, we'd lose water pressure for the hoses. The two lifeboats, and life rafts, were against the deckhouse, port and starboard side, at the mess deck level, two levels above the main deck. We'd be lucky to get clear, if we could get clear in these seas, before smoke and flames overwhelmed us. Christ, this had happened fast. The ship might remain afloat, but there was no place a person could survive while the fire raged.

I radioed the Canadian Coast Guard to report we had a ship fire. I gave them our position. We were one hundred miles from the nearest land, southwest of the Queen Charlotte Islands, too far for a helicopter rescue from the mainland, if that were even possible in these conditions. Then I called Bruce, at company headquarters, the Marine Division. I woke him and gave him the bad news: we had a fire and had to abandon ship. I gave our current navigational position.

"Halon discharged, captain. Engine room sealed. Fire on the main deck and in both tunnels." Randall sounded calm.

I sounded the alarm to abandon ship. I was crying, but this time not for Jimmie.

I watched the dials and gauges as the Chief began shutting down the main engine but leaving the generators going. The engine revolutions dropped to zero. In minutes, the ship would slew and begin to lose way.

"Get your boat teams to the boats now, Randall. Have people grab their survival suits and bring them, but be fast. Now. Don't even shuck your fire gear."

I coughed as the smoke grew thicker. The ship, wallowing, would track ahead for several minutes under its own momentum. I set the autopilot and left the bridge.

We were twenty souls, including the steward's department, engineers, deckhands, officers, and two Russian cargo minders. We had no time. I grabbed my wallet and personal logbook and struggled into my survival suit. The officers and engineers had cabins on the top decks and they had to climb the stairs to grab their survival suits, and I knew as I descended, passing Jim, chief engineer, and Fred, second mate, and Anne, the third mate, not everyone would have a chance to get their suits. Those in the heavy fire coveralls and jackets would have to settle for those and pray they didn't end up in the water. Smoke swirled in the stairwell.

The two boat crews gathered in the hallway running across the ship by the mess, each group separated by a few feet. Even in the smoke and the rising heat, we fell into habit from years of drills. The lead officer called attendance, making sure everyone was present, checking that lights on survival suits worked. Then, as the last names were read, the two teams separated, one headed to the starboard side, the other to the port side.

I was assigned to the port side boat along with Fred, the second mate, all the engineers except the Chief, Butch the wiper, Jamal the reefer, Harry the junior engineer, Richard the cook and the cook's helper, Raoul. The nine of us shuffled and walked in the smoke out onto the deck below the lifeboat and struggled up the steps onto the small platform where the boat hung. Two wore street clothes and were already shivering. The lifeboat was mounted on two big davits. A small platform led onto the stern of the boat. The lifeboats were designed as closed units, able to self-right once everyone straps in. Fred held open the door and people struggled to the benches running along each side in the interior, where they grabbed canvas belts and strapped in. The big ship rolled and smoke blew into the lifeboat. Below my feet, through the grating of the platform, I saw flames licking around the main deck doorway and I could see, inside through the windows to the mess, the flickering light of fire there, igniting the fats and grease in the traps in the galley.

Everyone boarded without saying a word. Finally, I climbed in and Fred, who was the boat leader during all our drills, closed the door. I strapped into the conning seat aft and started the engine. The engine caught the first turn. The conning seat was mounted over the engine, higher than the benches along the sides where the others were strapping in. Above me was a bubble with portholes, sticking out above the covered and curved deck of the boat. Through the streaked plastic portholes I saw rain and smoke.

"Everyone strapped in?" I asked Fred.

I watched him peer forward, but it was still dark in the boat because daylight was only beginning to show. I knew Fred couldn't see the others, but he nodded to me. The ship rolled and a huge sea passed just below us. In one instant, the crest of the wave was only ten feet below our keel, and in the next, we were hanging forty feet in the air. Looking out through a window in the steering bubble, I could see the burning ship was losing way and beginning her slew to port.

Everyone sat huddled in bulky survival suits or firefighting gear, eyes wide or shut tight. I grabbed the lever to let go the falls so our lifeboat could drop, and pulled. The boat dropped, fast. All my attention was in my ass, waiting for the slam as the next sea struck us as we dropped.

We first swung away from the ship when she rolled to port and then we struck the side of the ship when she rolled to starboard. Everyone shouted at the impact. I prayed the fall lines remained free as we spun down toward the water. The lifeboat struck the face of the next sea and pulled forward, still dropping, then rose as the sea gathered, then dropped again, suddenly, as the sea passed.

"Let go," I shouted, "Now."

Mark, the first engineer, pulled the release lever for the forward falls just as Fred pulled the lever for the stern falls.

Released, the boat dropped two feet and struck the water, hard. She was free and away and the engine was running. I steered to port, away from the ship.

Fred watched me like a hawk, trying to read from my eyes and body language how we were doing, because only I could see outside, through the steering bubble.

We were swept within five feet of the rusty, rolling side of the ship, but then the little engine grabbed water and I was able to veer away. We climbed huge seas as I struggled to get around the ship into the lee where the other lifeboat should be. I clawed off to the left as giant waves passed by, until I could head downwind past the bow. The sky was becoming brighter. I started looking for the other lifeboat once we crossed the bow.

"You reach the Coast Guard, Steve?" Fred was preparing the EPIRB – the Emergency Position Indicating Radio Beacon.

"I did. We'll have to head for nearest shore, meet a tow."

"That's the Charlottes."

"I know."

I could see the ship as we crossed the bow. She lay across the wind, billowing smoke. I saw flames leaping from the containers by number two hold. The deckhouse was pouring smoke from the main deck. We had dropped free with literally seconds to spare.

The ship rolled our way and I saw the tops of the stacked containers. The other lifeboat must have dropped because the davits were empty, but the lifeboat was nowhere to be seen. Then a rain shower came down and the ship was gone.

"Inventory, Second?"

Forward, two crewmen were already seasick. The lifeboat was like a cork in a stream, rolling and swinging, a motion totally unlike the long slow rolls of a ship. Vomit would gather in the bottom of the lifeboat and begin to stink, but by then we wouldn't notice because by then the boat bilges would contain feces and piss. We had no toilet. Nobody talked about this, but that's why we were supposed to bring hats – for those who refused to shit in their survival suits.

"EPIRB battery good and on. Radio battery seems good and you can try when you want. We just inventoried the water and food aboard this boat before Dutch. We've got four days of rations, but we gotta worry about the cold."

The water was warm out here in December, and the snow wasn't thick, but the air was still nearly freezing and the wind was strong. Within the lifeboat, we were protected from the wind but not the cold. The wiper and the reefer wore fire gear and all but two of the rest were in a survival suit. It would be close. If help could find us, once we got closer to land, we might be all right.

The engine throbbed. The huge seas lifted, then dropped. We were still in the lee of the ship. The seas would get worse as we moved away. I kept trying to spot the other lifeboat.

"Stay strapped in," Fred said. Harry the junior engineer was unstrapping his harness.

"I have to pee."

"Then pee where you are."

"Jesus."

Jamal threw up.

Perched on my raised seat above the engine, I stared ahead through the tiny windows. All I could see was water, spray, rain and snow. The seas were at least thirty feet high and came one after the other. I steered before the wind and hoped for the best. If help found us, they'd throw a line and we'd be towed for hours, if not days, behind a small tug or ship to sheltered waters, everyone in the lifeboat cold, seasick, and filthy. At least we'd be alive.

I toggled the small radio and began calling Randall in the other boat. The radio hissed. I kept calling. Our lifeboat corkscrewed and lunged. People lurched against their straps.

"Randall. First. You on? This is Boat One, vessel *Seattle Express*, radio check. Radio check . . . Radio check."

The radio remained silent.

"Maybe their radio's out," Fred was watching me closely. "That can happen."

Fred sailed second mate, had for years, but he was a Master like I was and he had sailed as Master when younger, and he knew what I was feeling. I looked at my watch. It was not yet nine in the morning. I was in a lifeboat, a lost ship burning behind me, half, no, more than half my crew very likely crushed or drowned or burned to death and the rest now sitting on the benches below me, strapped in, relying entirely on my leadership for survival.

You couldn't drill for this, not really, just as you couldn't really drill for combat or how you were going to handle being told by your doctor you had months to live.

It felt good to be able to smile, but none of this was amusing. I knew Butch, Jamal, and the young second engineer, Carl, all felt reassured the old man was sitting there, a smile on his face, assuming I was not concerned, and therefore they should not be concerned. I was plenty concerned, but if they wanted to feel better, more power to them.

The boat already stank.

Chapter Two
Louise

Louise woke, furious. She had known what was going on for weeks. She was going to dump Larry's ass, but Larry owned half the business and they were on the edge of collapse. If she threw him out, there'd be nothing left. Now he slept beside her, oblivious.

It had been a while since the two of them had had anything going in the bedroom. All business, all the time, and before that, being unable to have kids, then not wanting kids. Bills, breakdowns, and infrequent tows for *Warhorse* didn't do much for sex drive. But still, she had her pride. She was still a damn good-looking woman, if a little worn at the edges. Look at the way Travis, the cute wire splicer, had looked at her last year before he quit. He had the fire for her. Maybe she'd plan a revenge romp, she and Travis, aboard *Warhorse*, maybe in the wheelhouse.

Louise half smiled Then she imagined Larry with the puffy bimbo he'd met that Saturday in the casino. Hell, Louise had even been there, seen in an instant what was going to happen. She didn't give a shit, not anymore, but still, it hurt. Now, though, hearing the wind, she smelled money.

She got out of bed and padded over to the big window above the shop, looked out at the harbor. The wind carried sheets of rain across the harbor, stippling the surface. That's what Louise had smelled, money. She always smelled the money, had since she was a girl following her pop around. She had a nose for this, smelling the weather, knowing when the wind might bring them work.

Christ, they needed money. They had been here before, three times in the last six years. Each time the bank bridged them over. What choice did the bank have? No bank wanted a salvage operation way out on the Olympic Peninsula, especially just a worn out house, a tin shack, rusty cranes, and an ancient salvage tug. They had three acres at the head of tiny Sol Duc harbor, next to the marina, looking over at the port dock, the one the mining company had leased. Their land might have been valuable if not so contaminated, but so long as they didn't dig into beneath the surface, they could carry on, at least for a while.

When Louise's pop started the operation in the 1960s, they'd been closer than their rival salvage companies to the dangerous waters off British Columbia and Alaska. Even though old *Warhorse*, their tug, was slow, their strategic position along the Strait of Juan de Fuca meant they beat the bigger and faster tugs from Seattle and Vancouver rushing to meet foundering ships. In later years, the other tugs became faster, and fewer ships foundered. Louise and Larry were reduced to making difficult tows, sometimes cross-Pacific, babying *Warhorse* the whole way. Now even that had dried up. They had been barely hanging on. They'd been busy on a contract, scooping debris from the Elwha River as the dams were removed, but the work had ended when the rains began in October. There had been no work since. Now Larry had the gall to start an affair.

"We need a big claim," Louise spoke to the black window.

"What?" Larry rolled over, half asleep. He'd brought *Warhorse* back from the repair yard at Lake Union the day before, accompanied by her two brothers, Jeff and Vince. Jeff served as engineer and Vince as assistant engineer. *Warhorse* was old, built in 1952, but built to last. The Seattle yard had billed them $23,000, money they absolutely didn't have. But Bill from the bank rolled the charges and the loan payments another month, and he'd probably have to keep rolling the charges until the cleanup work started the following spring.

The dark harbor roiled beneath the rain and wind. Larry sat up, rubbing his eyes.

"You smell something, darlin? Money?"

Louise turned around. The room was dark, but Larry's big shoulders stood out against the headboard of the bed. He was still in damn decent shape for someone now 48. Had to be, horsing heavy gear around on the tug. Louise had liked it sailing with Larry — she had papers as a first mate — but then Larry's mother had taken ill and needed care. His mother had been the bookkeeper and Louise had to take over. When she wasn't in the office, she spent her time on the road around the Sound hustling work. She had to do a lot of hustling.

Larry still looked good. "Something woke me up." Now wasn't the time to get into a fight, and besides, Louise felt something in her bones. A metal pulley rattled against a post out on their dock. "*Warhorse* all tuned up, Larry?"

"Pushed us out of the yard before they really got into the shaft coupling repair, but I think we're OK. They rebuilt the winches, the big towing bit. New wire, too."

"Yeah, that's where eight of the twenty-three grand went. Hell."

"We need good wire, Louise, if we hope to snag anything."

Louise was facing Larry. If she wasn't so pissed at him she'd have climbed back into the bed.

She heard something on the radio they always left on. "Wait." She turned up the volume. She'd set up the receiver to scan all the distress channels, plus a couple of other companies used to send messages among themselves. Now she had picked up a transmission from Buckhorn headquarters to their big tugs down in Bremerton, west of Seattle. Louise prided herself on knowing what the competition did, and she knew the Buckhorn tugs had just hauled a decommissioned sub into the Bremerton Naval Yard where they were going to cut out the hot reactor core. The tugs were way down in the Sound, at least eight hours from Port Angeles, where they were usually based. "Listen."

The radio was scratchy but clear. "Sector Six. Open contract tow. Cast the sub after she's moored and get going. Yes, abandoned. Fire."

"There's something out there and Buckhorn's sending the big tugs." Louise was grinning.

"Sector Six is out in the Gulf of Alaska, west of the Charlottes." Larry turned on a light and examined a chart in the wall of their bedroom.

"They said fire, right?"

"I heard abandoned." Larry looked more closely at the chart.

"A long ways, Larry, more than five hundred miles. We'll have to pass outside Vancouver Island, it's faster but more exposed."

"It'll be plenty exposed out in Sector Six."

"What do you think is out there?"

"Ship. Something big, for them to send their tugs. Maybe one of their ships."

"Maybe the *Express*, Larry?"

"Could be." Larry pulled on his pants. "I'll call your brothers, see if we can get their cousins, too. We'll need ten, twelve guys, if we try this. I think you're gonna have to come, too, Louise. I need another mate, someone who can help Nelson handle the tug when I take the gang aboard the ship."

"If you can get on the ship. It's been a while, Larry."

"What else can we do? You going to sit here and wait? Get Jeff's wife to monitor the chatter. Have her find out where the ship was, where the Buckhorn tugs are. You don't need to be here. Right now we got to load up on a ton of food and get going."

"You have fuel? We'll need a lot of fuel."

"She's full. Been full too long, Louise."

"Gonna be a rough trip, Larry."

"*Warhorse* is built for rough trips."

"It's not *Warhorse* I'm thinking about. It's you, my brothers and cousins. Me."

"We'll be careful. I'll make the calls. You and your brothers, get food. Is the WalMart open this early? I'll call the rest of the gang, plus get some others."

"What? Who you going to get?"

"Dark Cloud's crew. They'll come, their tug's in the yard. They have no work either."

"They're crazy." Louise didn't like Dark Cloud. He'd taken business from *Warhorse* over the years. And what was it with his name, anyway? He was about as Native American as Louise was. But he knew what he was doing on a tug and they needed people who knew what they were doing.

"I'll even call Travis, bring him."

"He's a reporter now, Larry, for the Peninsula News; has been for a year."

"Best kid splicing wire I ever saw, Louise."

"Lotta food, Larry. Ten, twelve people."

Outside, the black night seemed lighter. Rain ran down the windows.

"Are we broke, Louise?" Larry, now dressed, was pulling on his boots.

"Broke as can be."

"Well, then. We want to be there first, we gotta get outa here, fast. Every hour here those big tugs are closer. They're a little faster than *Warhorse*, but not by much."

"What about the Canadian companies?" Louise knew Larry carefully watched what the Canadian salvors were doing.

"They'll be nosing around, but this time of year they're usually off in Asia working over there. Risk we must take. Those Buckhorn tugs worry me. If the *Express* caught fire and was abandoned, she's a Buckhorn ship and they'll want to grab her under their contract to avoid a big claim."

"We'll be in a race, Larry." Louise knew the Buckhorn people. Their tug operation was big and they thought they were the best. The Buckhorn captains looked down their noses at Larry and his crew, and they thought *Warhorse* was an ancient, useless scow. They even called Louise "Tugboat Annie" behind her back, which she was actually proud of. Over the years, *Warhorse* had brought in more prizes than any other two tugs in the United States, and her engines were still sound, her steel good.

Larry threw clothing into a bag for the tug and called her brothers. Louise made coffee. Ten minutes later Jeff and Vince appeared.

"What is it?" Jeff looked half asleep. He was rubbing his eyes.

"Don't know. Maybe the *Express*. Up off the Charlottes."

"Jesus."

No money in the bank, broke, string nearly run out. If they steamed north five hundred miles and missed the ship, or the ship was taken by the Buckhorn tugs, or if the ship sank, *Warhorse* would be out of fuel, out of money, and out of a future. If they somehow got a line on the ship first, claimed her, and brought her to a dock, they'd have a solid claim.

Louise knew she was going to get seasick once they got into the middle of the Strait. She always got seasick after spending months ashore. This time it had been years. First they had to find the ship. Then they had to get aboard. That was going to be the trickiest part, finding a way to get aboard a derelict vessel, dead in the water, almost certainly without a gangway or rope ladder down the side.

"We sure about this?" Larry asked at the front door. "All we heard was one transmission about the tugs, and the abandonment. If the captain's still aboard her we can't claim her by law."

"Larry, if she is really abandoned and is still afloat when you get there, you'll never have a head start like this again, because those tugs are usually at Port Angeles."

"Gonna be a nasty trip up there."

"Yes."

Larry donned some oilskins and headed down to the dock after calling the others to make a full crew. Louise got into her van with the brothers to get groceries.

The rain fell. The day was brightening. The wind was blowing, cold.

If you enjoyed this excerpt from Adrift, look for it this fall at bookstores or online.

Author Intro

EVA McGINNIS

My Polish parents were refugees, enslaved by Nazis during WWII. I was a toddler when we emigrated to the United States from Germany, and I spoke no English. My loving parents stressed education, and I thrived in the worlds that reading opened to me. During the years I struggled with thinking in two languages and cultures, patches of nature were places that I could find grace and freedom.

I hold degrees from Michigan State, Iowa State and a certificate in Poetry from University of Washington. Along the way, I've taught at Western Washington, run my own counseling practice, consulted with Boeing, and raised a family.

I am now enjoying my spiritual communities in Port Angeles and Sequim. I love conducting weddings and celebrations of all kinds as well as making glass bead jewelry with my husband. We can be found hiking, taking photos, and gathering mushrooms in our forests, as well as harvesting the abundant seaweed of our beaches.

Eva McGinnis is writing a third book of poetry to go with her first two, *Wings to my Breath* and *At the Edge of the Earth*, both available on Amazon.com. She has been published in several literary books and magazines, and can be reached at Evapoet@mcginnishome.org.

AFTERMATH WINTER STORMS ON THE OLYMPIC PENINSULA

Trunks of alders and fir
ravaged and splintered
like broken femur bones,
scattered alongside the twisted
elbows and gnarled knees.

Several firs wrenched
up by their roots
exposing their fragile tendrils
like pale private parts,
clinging hopelessly
to clumps of dark earth.

Stand of young trees
toppled, intertwined,
stood bravely
against the haughty winds,
stretching and swaying
their branch arms,
struggling to hold onto each other.

Perhaps the old survivors
whispered advice about
withstanding the hurricane
gusts rushing the valley,
"Bend and stay calm."
Not much could have saved those trees
clinging to the waterlogged slopes.

In my private requiem I wonder:
Does a tree feel pain when it's struck down?
When is it really dead?
Does it count, that I see
a tender fiddlehead poised to unfurl
its pale green body among the fallen branches?

Part 2

We clear the bones of my friends,
by renaming them "firewood."
My husband saws. I carry and stack
logs to the large pile by the road.
Thumping sound of wood landing
on wood reminds me of
bowling pins striking each other
at the end of an alley way,
clumsy days of teen dating.
It makes me smile.

Pushing the wheelbarrow full of logs,
I remember yesterday's conversation
with my friend
in a Georgia hospital,
I wish I could give her a day
in the spring woods
away from her cancer.

A neighbor and his dog stop by
on their walk down the road
eager to report the large cougar
tracks spotted up the mountain.
We experience the anticipation of
spotting him someday.

Later we spread a blanket
on the most level spot we can find
eat our sandwiches and split the cookie.
A tiny white butterfly appears and
fusses around us, like my mother used to do.
She would have loved this simple day
with its gentle fragrances,
promise of summer blossoms.
A frog bellows his greeting three times
somewhere in the woods.

ASTONISHMENT

Mother bird steps
into my woodland path
leading me away from
her nest, pretending an injured wing
as if I didn't see through her rouse.
She captures
my admiration
at her bravery,
taking on my giant form
for the sake of her family.

She reminds me of refugee parents
who cross waters in crowded flimsy rafts
hide in trunks of cars,
stumble over desert sands,
trusting coyotes
who may rob or enslave them
all for their children's survival.
Only to have their children
ripped from their arms at the border.

Yet some affluent others
abandon their offspring
as if they were fish eggs
that know how to swim from birth.

MISTS OF THE MOUNTAINS

Gossamer veils, transparent shrouds

mists drape over my tree encrusted mountains

softening my gaze, muting my steps

whispering of timelessness, soft endurance

blessing with fine sprays of holy water.

Is this where you walk now, beloved Mother,

free from fear of heights and false anchors?

Do you fly above mists or float inside them?

Will you encapsulate me again in your watery womb?

Or must I just dream, of our reunion

in the herbal sweetness of an imaginary heaven?

AUTUMN SNAPSHOTS

Two little girls in red sweatshirts
swing in tree branches
like barely ripe apples,
older sister teeters on lower limb,
dangles burgundy sneakers.
I gasp with a mother's instinct
when they all jump together
like a flock of birds responding
to a silent shotgun.
The tree gifts the air
with golden leaves
their laughter.

Across the street, young bridesmaids in burnt scarlet gowns
dazzling as puffy autumn dahlias
pose for photos on the pier.
A cool breeze quivers off the water,
sends shivers down their bare backs
as they wobble in unfamiliar strapless heels
to avoid the gaps in wooden planks.
Handsome groomsmen willingly oblige
with protective arms around the girls,
thrilled with the need for warmth in such
fine company.

Below the pier,
three Morning Sun starfish
stretch abundant scarlet arms
over rocky bottom at low tide,
while a maroon scallop
sensitive to their deadly embraces
hiccups out of the way
rippling the water
on a perfect ruby day in the park.

FOREST MAGIC – MT. PLEASANT
ETERNAL JULY

Weary of city soot I left behind two hours ago,
I stumble on a speckled rock
along the wooded path to the Big Tree.
It leaps into the air – a frog.
I bend down to apologize.

While nearer the ground, I observe
a newly erupted mushroom
standing on its one thin leg,
headful of dirt and needles.

In a sunny spot along the trail,
a curved stick slithers away as I approach.
This time I sidestep quickly,
but the snake retreats even faster
into the underbrush. Not far, a thistle
sports a pink flower adorned
with a hovering bee.
I photograph the bee, which I would
have chased away in the city.

Along the path there are openings where
I hear the echoing rush of the river
in the valley. I play with choosing to hear
its music first as foreground then as background.
I'm thrilled that it's not the dull roar of city traffic,
which I used to filter, by pretending it was a river,
Otherwise I would go crazy with its drone.
Here my river holds many songs!

When I reach the clearing, I spread my blanket
remove my boots and socks,
gingerly stepping on moist dirt.
I watch my toes scoop up soft pine needles.
I relinquish control to the "small animal"
of my body. I am quickly on all fours,
stretching, then on my back
and my hands open towards the sun.
When my mind quiets,
I pull out my journal and write
away my disappointments and
fill up on gratitude for this moment.

On this mountain I feel nurtured
by the sky and wind, which can conspire
to birth rain clouds from pure blueness
in under an hour. This day an angel cloud
floats by and leaves me blessed.

On the way back,
I see the split second leaps of a wild rabbit
across my path and the quick flicker
of the deer's tail as she warns
her two fawns of my coming.
All three disappear completely
into the thick underbrush in a breath's time.
I stand blinking with disbelief.

I follow after them, but the third inner tree
stops me, with its signage of stripped bark
and encircling deep claw marks. My friends
warned me that both bears and cougars have
been spotted nearby this summer. Here are
their glyphs. I put my fingers in
the deep groves and trace them down the tree
in awe of the strength that carves into living wood.
But I venture no further.

Back on the path,
I breathe in the forest magic,
with creatures that shape shift
and messages strewn
in rocks, sticks and sky.

JANUARY SOUNDS BENEATH THE SILENCE
Mt. Pleasant Woods

The long-hidden sun alights on my upturned face,
like mother's touch on the cheek of her child,
who has trekked home through near darkness.
I want to believe that the worst of the cold is over.

In the shadow, two large footprint-shaped patches of snow,
embellished with pine needles and stray alder leaves,
stand witness to last month's surly storm.
Nearby, maple leaves lay stitched by sequined frost.

Where the sun transmutes the snow,
water seeps up to the spongy surface
nourishes virile sword ferns,
newly liberated from the weight of winter's blanket.

In the deep woods, slick shelf fungi
ring the spruce, like twirling skirts.
Bright orange of witch's butter mushroom
silently sings bold volumes of hope.

Downed branches in the clearing
laced together with slender spider threads,
glisten and catch rainbows inside themselves,
weave forest to sky.

On the periphery of my vision,
spirits of forest ancestors
encapsulated in transparent light orbs,
gently glide among the branches.

When I lower myself onto a downed log,
my thoughts into a sweet hollow,
I can almost hear sap rising
inside moss-covered skins of firs.

The wind, messenger of the river
brings trills from the throat of a tiny tree frog,
a love song for these woods, and for the planet,
awakening codes of Light.

LONE DUCK IN WETLANDS

Last week,
fussy and clucking,
she was surrounded
by eight fuzzy chicks.
They barely kept up with her,
as they jostled each other, noisily,
while she steered them away from
my shadow which stretched,
to the water's edge.
I marveled at her marshalling style.

Today, she is alone,
on the broad tree stump
in the middle of the boggy pond,
perched one-legged,
head tucked into her feathers
like a yoga master balancing
her low-slung body
in perfect pose.

I zoom my camera lens
to search for her little chicks,
I wait and scan again and again.
But none appear.

I check for the nonchalant heron
who often stands in the reeds
on the other side of the water.
Did she scoop the ducklings
to take to her babies' nest?
She is not there today.

I also suspect ravens
whom I witnessed
harassing another mother duck
and her klatch of chicks
at low tide of the bay, two days ago.
I had intervened there, momentarily,
shooing the ravens away from the chicks.

I'd like to pretend
that instead of an early demise,
these ducklings were a fast-growing breed
that flew from home,
too quickly, perhaps,
leaving her standing on her one mother leg,
to catch up on her sleep.

In her stillness
is there grief or resignation?
Do her bird dreams protect her?
Her instincts absolve and reassure her?

Perhaps, my sadness for her children
is my own sleepless worry
over my lone chick,
flown, so young,
to a distant pond.

A cool breeze envelopes me,
like my mother's whisper.
I feel her presence
and sigh with understanding,
this is how my mother felt at my flight too.

I am not alone,
and in that, there is peace.
I nod my thanks to the lone duck
as she lifts her head
and stretches her wings,
the sun at our backs.

SPRING – THEN AND NOW

I have read that trees send messages
to each other on the wind.
In my neighborhood, this late March week,
they must have all agreed -
Ready. Set. Send out shoots, now!

How does it happen?
Rough branches on my apple tree
spill out clusters of angel-pink blossoms,
burst into leaves –
tender in new greenness.
As a child, I broke up sticks looking
for the flowers inside, certain I had
only to find the right ones.

What about the pussy willows?
Where did all that fur come from?
Had the ground been collecting
lint from the air all winter
to sprout such little tufts?
As a child, I stroked my cheek with them
dreaming that these were the true magic wands.

Can you fathom those lilacs?
They must have simmered perfume
in some underground pockets of my backyard,
at the ready, to spray it, now
so generously into the breeze.
As a child, I smelled the ground
beneath the giant lilac bush,
searching for the secret juices.

Today I look at the turquoise backdrop of sky
from under the bouquets
of redbud tree blossoms.
The wind, a lover, embraces us.
A petal falls past my shoulder,
a whispered benediction
of miracles I will never understand.

SUMMER REFLECTIONS BY LAKE CREEK

Chanting river pebbles
whisper invitation…
Come,
Step in,
Stay.

I gingerly slide my feet
into mountain's glacial milk,
swift current slices cold into my bones
thrilling silver notes up my spine,

I stroke emerald skullcap
of giant mossy rock at creek's edge
sponge up its moisture
through my pores.

Berry-scented wind strokes my hair,
tugs at my brusque edges,
till I breathe with water's
pulsing rhythm.

Silent deer track my movements
ears twitching, tails signaling
on opposite shore.

As I soften my vision below the surface,
boulders etched into shapes of seals
stare back from under the water.
What do you want?

Giant maple leaf spirals gently on the breeze
lands in eddy than flips and escapes,
finds strong central undercurrent
to carry us home.

Author Intro

MELEE MᴄGUIRE

I am a high school counselor by day and budding novelist by night, and weekends, and holidays. I have lived in Sequim for the last four years, and it's the first place in fourteen moves that hasn't got me packing boxes again. My husband and I love living in such an amazing community where our passions are empowered. We have two beautiful girls, and we are looking forward to being empty nesters (parents of teenagers, you know what I mean). I am currently working on a new full length novel and hope to one day see my books on a bookstore shelf, or in the hands of a stranger sitting at a coffee shop.

You can reach Melee at melee.mcguire@gmail.com.

MOVES LIKE A KNITTER

He'd been watching her for a few weeks now. She settled herself onto the hard plastic bench seat of the ferry, putting her coffee on the table in front of her and pulling her knitting free from the cloth bag. She sat with her back to the window and its beautiful views of the Puget Sound and Seattle's iconic skyline. Watching the city grow larger as the ferry moved closer always made Sarah grateful. Her life held beautiful landscapes and several close friends. It was more than she expected. More than she deserved by far.

But today she didn't look at the choppy waters of the Sound or Mount Rainer's impressive crags covered in snow, disappearing into white clouds. She angled her body so she could watch him, as he watched her. A coy hide and seek of eye contact. In another life, another time, she might consider this flirting. But the adrenaline coursing through her veins had nothing to do with sexual intent, although the man was striking. Dark hair that curled to the high collar of his slate-green knit sweater. Eyes that might be blue, might be something darker. He sat on the far side of the galley, nursing his own cup of coffee. The distance was too great to make out finer details. Like the scar that cut through his left eyebrow, or the inky shadow of stubble from a missed shave that morning. But she could imagine these intimate facts, see them in her imagination as clear as the fibers of her yarn.

She shifted in her seat, letting her hands busy themselves with her needles and wool. It was going to be a chunky scarf and her needles were almost comically large. Knit one, purl two. The pattern was simple and didn't require real concentration, but if he happened to look her way, she could glance down and appear engaged.

"People will think you are obsessed."

The voice of her closest friend echoed in her mind. She was right. Sarah was a bit obsessed with the man. And his notice of her. Why would he do that? Day after day, surreptitious glances that lingered. It was odd. She was not ugly. Men found her attractive when she tried. But she wasn't trying. If anything, she tried to disappear, safe and unnoticed in a sea of people. And still, he watched her. It was disconcerting.

Not as disconcerting as when he stood. His eyes stayed steady on her, even when she made it clear that she noticed him. He started walking towards her and her hands fumbled. She dropped a stich and cursed quietly. Looking down at her knitting, she waited for his heavy boots to pass her. She could feel his presence, dark and angry energy drawing closer. But that was just her fanciful imagination running away with itself.

Get it together, Sarah.

Holding her breath, she counted to ten. She did that as a child when the monsters clawed outside her bedroom door. Count to ten and they'll disappear. Unless they didn't. Unless they beat down the door and came looking under the covers for what shivered and quaked.

Looking up, she expected to see a clear path leading past the rows of tables and chairs in the galley, towards the back of the ferry. Instead, her eyes fell upon the slate-green knit sweater. This close, she could see that it stretched a bit over a well-defined chest. She lifted her gaze higher and could say with confidence his eyes were blue. Dark and deep and narrowed in what she could only assume was carefully controlled anger.

"May I?" He indicated the seat opposite her and before Sarah could respond, he sat. Only the table separated them. It seemed a woefully inadequate barrier. He was much bigger this close. Much harder.

"I, um. Sure. I guess. I mean, actually no. That seat is taken." Sarah tightened her grip on the knitting needles and shifted in her seat so her left leg was bent, the heel of her foot pressed against the seat. She could scramble up in a moment, leap into the aisle if she needed to make a quick escape.

"Really. I don't see anyone sitting here." His voice was a deep rumble and the ire simmering in his eyes echoed in his words.

"I think you should leave." Her voice was low and steady. She risked a glance behind him and saw two men in business suits looking over with interest, or perhaps the beginning of concern.

"I think you should tell me who the hell you are and what you're doing on this ferry."

Sarah recoiled from him, her eyes widening. "Excuse me? I should tell you who I am? Who the hell are you? I'm not telling you anything."

"You've been watching me. For weeks. You think I haven't noticed? Are you from the government? Private sector? What?"

The hairs along Sarah's arm prickled to life and she could feel her heartbeat accelerate. "I don't know what you're talking about. I'm a knitter. I work at So Much Yarn in Pike Market." Sarah held up her knitting needles with the newly started scarf hanging haphazardly. "See?"

He took a deep breath and Sarah tried not to notice the muscles in his jaw jump and dance as he clenched his teeth. "Why should I believe you?"

"Seriously? Why shouldn't you believe me? Frankly, of the two of us, I have way more cause for alarm than you. What kind of crazy man sits down at a stranger's table and starts accusing them of being government? What does that even mean? Are you running for some office and worried about your competition?"

"You don't move like a knitter."

Sarah couldn't stop the full throated laugh that erupted. She shook her head. "I don't *move* like a knitter? How does one move when one knits?"

Her laughter only seemed to increase his frustration. "That's not what I meant. I mean you move like you've had training."

Sarah's brows drew together and a lick of fear flamed along her nerve endings creating pricks of sensation in her armpits and behind her knees. "I think you need to leave."

He sat silent, his eyes burning into hers.

Breaking the impromptu staring contest, Sarah looked behind him and noticed the two business men were still watching them, one shifted in his seat as he unbuttoned his coat and loosened his tie a fraction.

"Fine." The man stood, his legs flexing in dark jeans. Sarah tried not to notice. He had powerful legs. He could probably jump across the width of a ferry with legs that strong. Not that it mattered. "Fine. I'll go. But tell your people I'm not for sale."

Sarah watched him retreat and refused to acknowledge the man's ass. She didn't notice its shape or the fact that his jeans covered him like a second skin. She didn't wonder, however fleetingly, what it might feel like to dig her fingers into the taut muscle as he pressed her hard against a wall. *I need to get out more, maybe start dating. This is unacceptable.*

Sarah loosened her grip on her needles and pulled free more yarn from the ball still sitting in her bag. Knit one, purl one.

The man sauntered past the two gentlemen in business suits. They watched him warily, obviously attuned to his negative energy. One of the men turned to her and nodded in a friendly fashion, his smile seemed forced. Sarah nodded back but didn't try to smile. Hers would have definitely been fake.

The man didn't sit in his original seat. He continued walking, heading towards the restrooms. Sarah took a deep breath, but her momentary calm was interrupted when both of the men in business suits stood and followed each other to the bathroom.

Odd.

The thought whispered through her mind and she was on her feet, slipping the stiches off her needles, bundling the scarf back into her bag and walking briskly towards the men's restroom.

The seats nearest the door to the men's restroom were all full of people. A mother sat with her toddler watching the water and looking for 'se-ows'. A woman wearing Armani shoes and a fitted jacket tapped quickly on her laptop. An older couple were working on one of the jigsaw puzzles left out by the ferry crew. A young man in maroon jeans and a grey hoody sprawled out on the bench seat nearest the restroom door, fast asleep.

Sarah didn't hesitate. She didn't give anyone time to notice her actions. She pushed through the bathroom door like nothing was amiss. No one seemed to register the woman with knitting needles who walked into the men's restroom.

A hand-dryer was on her right and to the left was a trough of metal urinals. Beyond them was a counter and five sinks. Thankfully both the urinals and sinks were empty. Sarah continued straight towards the stalls that were in a second room.

Ducking down, she counted shoes. Eight shoes equaled four men which was one man too many. Sarah recognized the scarred work boots. There were three pairs of shined up loafers but only one was a brand name and he was in the stall closest to the entrance that lead back to the urinals and sinks. She would have to be quick and quiet. Strolling past that stall, she continued five doors farther along the line and opened the stall next to Cheap Shoes Number One. Work boots was next to him and Cheap Shoes Number Two was on the other side. Based on the position of their feet, none of the men were sitting and it would be rather difficult to pee into the toilet with feet pointed towards the door.

The distinct sound of a wet fart rolled through the stalls, echoing off tiled floors. Sarah repressed the urge to gag. Men could be so gross. From the sound of the fart, it came from fancy feet in the far stall.

Doesn't matter how expensive your shoes, money never buys class. Just gas. Sarah smirked at her own joke.

She let one of her knitting needles slip down her right palm until the flat head rested against the heel of her hand. Pressing a small button on its shaft, the head expanded into a handle she could grip, and the tip of the needle extended to a blade. She took a deep breath. She didn't have time to count to ten, so she settled on three.

One, two, three.

One fluid movement placed her right foot on the toilet seat, her left on the back wall. She twisted and gripped the partition with her free hand to swing over coming down behind Cheap Shoes Number One. She noticed his hair was beginning to thin at his crown as she brought the blade down in a deadly jab that severed his spinal cord, cut his trachea and jugular and exited below his Adam's apple. He was dead before he could make a sound.

Sarah wrapped her left arm around his chest before he could slump to the floor and held him for a moment, listening. Another wet fart ripped through the bathroom creating a helpful, if disgusting, cover for any small noise she may have made. Working Boots in the stall next to her shuffled his feet and exhaled in a disgusted huff of breath.

My thoughts exactly Sarah settled the dead man against the toilet seat, hitting the flusher for good measure.

One down. One to go.

Work Boots exited his stall and Sarah waited to hear the door of the second business man. Cheap Shoes Number Two. As soon as the door creaked Sarah unlocked her stall and stepped out. Cheap Shoes already had his gun out.

"I wouldn't do that if I were you. That's a really nice sweater, such a pretty green. It would be a shame to ruin it." Sarah did smile this time.

The man in the green knit sweater turned and his deep blue eyes widened in surprise. "What ..."

Before he could ask his question the distinct sound of the outer door opening caused all three of them to freeze. They could hear the footsteps of a man walking to the urinal. Sarah took advantage of the momentary distraction, pushed Work Boots aside and kicked hard with her leg, aiming for Cheap Shoes' knees while grabbing his wrist and twisting hard, keeping the business end of his gun pointed up and away. She heard the crack of his knee cap as it shattered. It was the only sound he made before she thrust her blade up, through his throat as he fell. It was an exact mirror of the death blow she delivered to his partner, entering where her last had exited, below his Adam's apple and exiting at the base of his neck. He had brown eyes. They dimmed as he slumped to the floor.

The silence in the bathroom was broken only by the sound of the urinal being flushed in the other room and the echo of shoes exiting the bathroom.

Turning, Sarah looked up at the man with his deep blue eyes and curling black hair. "That is how a knitter moves. And you were right. I've had some training."

Author Intro

GORDON ANDERSON

I've camped all around the Olympic Peninsula as well as the Washington and Oregon coast. I think I drink too much coffee; I've had my library card for seventy years; I like to visit our national parks; I'm happiest near seawater. And, oh yes, I love to write poetry and prose. I use many different formats of poetry, composing free verse as well as verse with rhymes, haiku, tanka and tritina. I write a short story now and then.

My five books include three volumes of *Gordito Haiku, Chosen Poems: Words of Love* (a collection of love poems); *Looking Through the Knothole* (tritina style poems). I am about to publish my sixth book *Morning Coffee* which is a volume of free verse.

Gordon's books are available at www. echospringspub.com and on Amazon.com. He can be reached at dreamsandthoughtsga@gmail.com.

HAIKU

In Dawn's early light
through my window a blue heron
—it has to be spring

The coastline calls her
back out to Cape Alava
—to smell sea water

Watching gray whales
from Ruby Beach sea cliff
—breaching and blowing

With new leaf and bloom
she walks an Olympic trail
—her ritual each spring

In the rainforest
she prayed at a waterfall
for understanding

Autumn on the Hoh
he strolls in sun and shade
—living a good dream

In giant kelp beds
among floating brown ribbons
—otters and sea lions

Royal Basin falls
—all tumbling white-blue ribbons
on their downward flights

NO HUMPBACK PINKS

Up here in God's Country
on an Elwha bend
out on a sand bar
at the very end
—I've got my fishing tackle
I'm basking in the sun
enjoying the good weather
and the salmon run

As the crow flies
I flick my pole west
—my lure hits the water
and I'm hoping for the best
—to hook a nice silver
maybe even a big King
but I don't want no bony squawfish
or no humpback pinks

It's that time of year again
the fish are on the spawn
—I hope I catch a big one
the salmon run is on
but I don't want no humpback pinks
—they're just food for my dog
—I'm hoping for a big fat King
at least three feet long.

WILD SALMON

Wild salmon
getting messed with
in the creeks and streams
throughout this land
contamination—pollution

Too many people
with their fragmentations
and no fusions or unity
—no singleness of purpose
when it comes to salmon

Wild Salmon
destructing and crumbling
and now—fast disappearing
due to lack of unanimity
and no common cause

Too many factions
with no single-mindedness
instead—finger pointing
and multiple ministries
impacting salmon

Wild salmon
endangered—threatened
—in much need of help
across this country
with no united protector

Too many independents
concerned with self-interest
—where is the champion
where is the louder voice
to rescue wild salmon?

Where is—
the consolidated everyone
with the urgent action needed
to save wild salmon?

MY WINTER'S NEST

By my campfire's warmth
I sit and watch the storms
I am high and dry in my nest
in Olympic National Forest
up above the driftwood beach
on my yearly retreat

I hear the sea roar tonight
big waves are in my sight
as the vast ocean comes
on its rolling pounding drums
under moon and stars guiding light
—how I feel nature's might
as I watch the white caps leap
and breach—then waves
tumble to the beach

I am at my winter's nest
once again in rain and snow
just like years of old
—the trees with white
and winter's cold
—this atmosphere to me
in some wanting way
a needed getaway
—a pleasing comfort zone
where I sense a touch of home
on my cliff at Kalaloch Beach
at my winter's nest

I feel those strong coastal winds
as a new storm moves in
off the North Pacific's blow
where the tall evergreen trees grow
—when Mother Nature comes to call
all the mountains feel her squall

In the morning I will wake
to a foggy rainy dew
—but by the early noon
the sun will come shining through
the shore will become busy
with many birds and me
—us immersing the day
finding memories
while walking the beach

When thunder roars
then lightning flashes
and onto the beach
the ocean dances
swell after swell
the high waves roll in
under full moons
and clouded suns
my Kalaloch winter
does begin

I am at my winter's nest
once again in rain and snow
just like years of old
—the trees with white
and winter's cold
—this atmosphere to me

in some wanting way
a needed getaway
—a pleasing comfort zone
where I sense a touch of home
on my cliff at Kalaloch Beach
at my winter's nest.

ANOTHER DAY BEGINS

Another day begins
with a sunrise
and cock's crow
—a new dawn returns with daybreak
with the first light of the rising sun
—then from east to west the sun runs
throughout the morning
and early part of the day
to reach high noon

There the sun is far up
in the middle of the sky
where it becomes a noonday sun
and rests awhile
then travels through the afternoon
where shadows start to play
and daylight soon fades
into a short twilight
that turns to sundown dusk

It is then and there
—evening turns into the end of day
the sun disappears
and nightfall and darkness arrive
to linger for hours
along with shining moon and stars
until the night's end
and a new dawn's presence comes
with a mighty sunrise
and the cock's crow
as another day begins.

WHALES PASS TATOOSH
The Way It Was

Gray whales were migrating
they passed Tatoosh Island
and the murres and puffins
—they passed the tribal longhouses
out on the Cape

One early morning in May
a young boy
among some vagrant gulls and crows
is first on the beach
—he stands watching out at sea
from the Neah Bay shoreline

At sea in three carved cedar boats
the Makah are at steady paddle
—hunting the gray whale
just off the coast
and in the mouth of the Strait—somewhere

By afternoon more people came
below the rocks to the beach
to watch and wait with the boy
—then sightings were made
and the word was out—a whale had been caught

The hunters were bringing in a whale
—a giant forty foot gray whale
and but for the old aged ones in the village
all the Makah tribe was heading for the beach
in pleasurable excitement

All three eight-men crews
were moving through the water
as the canoes came into sight
—paddling with their many seal skin floats
and their sinew lines tight
—them pulling the great whale to the beach

The strong yew harpoon with its sharp tip
had met it's mark along with the lances
—the dead whale did not sink—and it lay on the beach
most all the Makah village performed a ceremony
to welcome the whale's spirit

Everyone was happy
the dogs barked and the people sang and danced
—the harpooner spread eagle feathers upon the whale's body
—then all the villagers began to cut and section up
the meat and oil into the night

The sunset came—and under the moon
big night fires burned along the beach
—later on in the week a big potlatch was given
where the leaders divided up the gray whale
with all of the tribal members

The boy eleven at that time
is today an old man
—it is May again—and the gray whales are migrating
and they pass Tatoosh Island
this time—he will be in a canoe paddling and hunting them
out beyond the Cape and tribal longhouses.

Author Intro

KIMBERLY MINARD

When I was ten, I wrote a tangled mess of a story involving a detective, a stuffed animal, and cheese. I like to think my writing has improved over the last thirty years, much like the cheese in that first story. These days, I teach high school English online and write fiction after hours until my eyes cross or I drool precariously close to the keyboard. Living in Sequim for the past six years has taught me the beauty of blackout curtains, the deliciousness of apple pancakes, and the need to drive under the speed limit. My supportive husband and lovely daughter put up with my writer's block, inept napping skills, and forgetfulness all while keeping me sane.

Kimberly can be reached at aknittedfrenzy@gmail.com

KNOCK

"Hi sweetie."

Camilla blinked sleepy eyes and found herself looking into her mother's. Her clear green eyes. Camilla's eyes. The two women smiled. Her mother placed her hand over Camilla's and squeezed. Camilla squeezed back.

"Hi mom." Camilla took in her surroundings wondering how she came to dream herself into this place. Camilla could almost name it but it was just out of reach. They sat at a rough-planked table. A table for eating. And seating a large number of eaters. A table Camilla knew and loved. Mismatched cushions tied to each seat with frayed ribbons in all the colors of the rainbow. Floral printed wallpaper covered every inch of the four walls. A window let in weak sunlight. Morning light. Two steaming mugs of strong coffee wafted under her nose.

"Cream?" her mother asked, lifting a tiny ceramic pitcher. Camilla nodded. Her mother poured a second's worth of cream into each mug. They both sipped. Warmth spread throughout Camilla. She couldn't shake the dream fog though. Am I dreaming?

"Where are we?" Camilla asked. She noted the plates attached to the walls and the floral curtains on each window in the living room. Framed photos filled the walls. Some faces looked familiar. The house felt familiar. Like an old friend or family member.

"Don't you recognize this place?" Her mother drank more coffee, her eyes never leaving Camilla's bewildered face.

"I do but I can't . . ." Camilla started. "It can't be, can it?" Her great-grandmother's farm house. The place she and her mother stayed for weeks or months at a time during Camilla's summer breaks from school. The creaky attic on the third floor she'd never dared to go into even once. The claw foot bathtub filled to the edge with bubbles every night. The cupboard under the first floor stairs where she read library books for hours with a flashlight. The tiny bedrooms with fluffy pillows Camilla sank into for afternoon naps. All the photo albums she could devour along with endless chocolate chip walnut cookies and milk.

"But I thought Gigi lost the farm."

Her mother shrugged. "Do you remember coming here during the summer time?" she asked.

"How could I forget?" Once a few memories slipped in, her mind overflowed with them. The hours-long drive from Spokane through the dry land, across the Sound on a ferry, eventually on the old highway to the Olympic Peninsula built the anticipation in Camilla's quaking body. She'd stick her head out the window to smell the salty air from the Strait of San Juan de Fuca as they drove closer to Sequim, Washington.

Camilla would jump out of the car before the tires stopped completely on the gravel drive and run into her waiting Gigi's arms. The overgrown backyard enticed Camilla to skip, twirl, cartwheel, and dance as soon as her bare feet touched the grassy expanse surrounded by fir trees and cedars. Berry vines overtook the back end of the yard and Camilla ate her fill every day of blackberries, raspberries, and salmonberries.

Even now, seeing berries in the grocery store rushed those summer days back to her. Her childhood spent frolicking. But Gigi couldn't keep up with the old house. Before Camilla turned ten, the farmhouse and all its loveliness was sold. And Gigi passed away the following year in the little condo she'd purchased with what savings she'd had left.

"At least, that's what I remember," Camilla said.

"Close," her mother said. "Gigi sold because no one in the family moved in to take care of the house."

"Why didn't we?" Camilla asked. "I loved it here."

Her mother nodded. "You did. So did I. But do you know why we spent so much time here during the summer?"

Camilla's selfish childish memory bank wouldn't let her see past the store of happy bliss she'd saved up.

"Why?" she finally asked.

"We were broke. Usually by the end of the school year, the money for rent was gone or I'd lost another job. We needed a place to stay. Gigi never judged." Camilla's mother's eyes glistened. "She welcomed us every year. Unlike my own mother."

"Nana? Nana judged you? Why?"

"For not quite following in her footsteps. For having you so young. For not finishing my education." She shrugged and sipped her coffee.

A voice from the kitchen called out. "I judged her because she wasted herself." Camilla's Nana walked into the dining room carrying her own cup of coffee.

Camilla jumped up to hug her Nana. She breathed in her familiar cherry almond scent and held on a few seconds longer. Nana patted Camilla's back with her free arm. "How's my girl?" Nana asked.

Camilla nodded, still holding on to her Nana. "You're here." But why? Despite the friction between mother and daughter, Camilla never felt anything but devotion from her Nana. Camilla and her mother moved addresses every year in Spokane. They bounced from apartment to mother-in-law unit to apartment throughout Camilla's childhood. But Nana stayed in the same mobile home park in Sequim. "Manufactured home, thank you," Nana would sniff. "Cost effective and less upkeep."

Though her constancy marked Camilla's childhood as well, Nana never invited her daughter and granddaughter to live with her full-time.

"Why was that, Nana?" Camilla finally pulled away from her Nana, thin under her sweater set and ever-present strand of fake pearls.

"Because I refused to be a crutch for your mother."

Camilla sat back down and picked up her coffee cup, still hot.

"Yes, darling Camilla, your mother could have been so much more." Camilla's mother sounded sad and filled with something familiar to Camilla. Regret.

"But Mom," Camilla placed her hand on her mother's hand. A study in aging, those hands. Half the age of her mother, her hands didn't bear the fine lines and sunspots her mother's did. "You were exactly who I needed you to be."

Nana snorted across the table. She took a seat. "That's lovely, Camilla, but not particularly useful. She should've finished high school and gone to college. Like I did. She wasted her brain on those menial jobs."

Camilla's mother nodded. "Yes. I should've gone back to school. And maybe I still will. Someday."

Nana shook her finger at her oldest daughter. "That's the kind of thinking that got you nowhere. Maybe. Someday." Nana shook her head and reached for the pitcher of cream.

"She could've answered the door." Another voice familiar to Camilla wafted in from the kitchen along with the smell of chocolate chip walnut cookies.

Nana looked up. Camilla's Aunt Rose, her mother's sister, entered the room with a plate of cookies, still warm from the oven.

"Hiya Camilla." Aunt Rose smiled at her only niece and circled the table to give Camilla a big shoulder squeeze. She sat in the chair to Camilla's right. Camilla stared. Aunt Rose too?

"Answered the door?" Camilla couldn't help asking, bewildered as she was to be surrounded by the women in her family. When have we ever been altogether like this?

"There was a knock after she had you and she ignored it." Aunt Rose bit into a cookie. Warm chocolate stuck to her chin. Camilla watched her aunt wipe the chocolate off with her finger and lick it before saying anything.

"And you answered the knock, Aunt Rose?" Camilla reached for a cookie.

Aunt Rose nodded her head. "You know the story though." She smiled. "Went to college. Majored in journalism. Wrote for the Times. The End."

"Writing for a major newspaper is no small potatoes, Rose." Nana raised her still steaming mug to her youngest. "Nor is winning the Pulitzer." Nana smiled.

Camilla's mother sat still staring into her mug. "I would've missed out on so much of Camilla if I'd opened the door. So much." Regret hung on the edges of her words.

"You'd have a name too, wouldn't you?" Nana asked. "Not just 'Camilla's mother.' You can be a mother and still have a name. I did. I do." Nana not only graduated from college in four years from the University of Washington with a double bachelor's in communication and philosophy, she then went on to earn her master's in counseling and started up her own counseling practice.

Camilla looked at her mother. Her Nana. Her Aunt Rose. Camilla finished high school after giving birth to Liam her senior year. She'd managed that much through the alternative school in Spokane. But since then, she'd held a series of barista and waitressing jobs.

Lately, she worked at a popular coffee shop downtown, Blue Mountain. Restaurants didn't always stick around in the small Pacific Northwest town. Folks seemed to think opening up an eatery meant printing up slick menus and bringing in weekend bands. But the townspeople of Sequim demanded good food and even better service. Bad reviews flew around faster than writing up the night's specials.

"Did I miss the knock?" Camilla said. In the midst of scraping by with Liam, her beautiful boy, she couldn't recall having ever heard what her aunt and Nana heard.

"You've already broken the chain by having a boy."

Camilla must have looked confused because Nana continued. "Do you know how long it's been since the Olsen line saw a boy in its ranks?" The maternal line of Olsen. Her last name. Her mother's. Nana. Aunt Rose.

"A while, I'm guessing." Camilla bit into a cookie. Still warm. Gooey chocolate hit her tongue like an old friend. The right amount of salt and crunch from the walnuts. Camilla savored each bite.

"At least six generations, according to Gigi's records in the family bible." Nana also reached for a cookie.

The family bible. The enormous tome Camilla would pore over for hours. The genders of the generations didn't stick with her.

"No boys. No husbands?" Camilla looked at each woman in the room. "No husbands. Any of you. Me." She stared at each of them. "What are we? Witches?" Liam's father took off when the second pink line showed up on her one and only pregnancy test. The summer before Camilla's senior year, the man-child headed off to backpack his way through the castles and graveyards of Europe. Nary a postcard or collect call from him since. Before the backpacker, Camilla's love life didn't exist. He was it. And he was gone.

"Some mighta said so, back in my day." An unfamiliar voice called out from the kitchen. Footsteps grew nearer. "I had a husband though! He gave me four girls. And then died when he was thirty-five and our youngest was six months old. Probably couldn't handle all that estrogen."

A woman with the hereditary Olsen green eyes smiled at Camilla and stood next to Nana. They shared the same smile. Nana stood to hug her mother. Camilla noticed the two women were the same height.

"Hi momma." Nana's momma. Gigi. Her white hair swept back from her lined tanned face into a thick bun. And her hands were tucked into a striped apron. Those hands cared for five daughters, built fences on the farm, and cooked every meal in the very kitchen she just emerged from.

Camilla stood and reached for her Gigi. "Hello," she said, near to tears. Her Gigi still smelled of roses and a touch of brown sugar. She squeezed back, not saying a word until she broke the hug. Camilla sat down in disbelief.

"My girls," Gigi said, her voice low and almost reverential. A smile played at the corner of her unadorned mouth. Nana gave up her seat and her mother took it. She looked at Camilla, her green eyes crinkling. "My sweet great-granddaughter. We aren't witches but we are reminders. Each one of us." She nodded to Camilla's mother, Aunt Rose, Nana. "We're reminders to answer that knock when it comes."

"But I ignored it. It must've already come and I ignored it. If I'd answered the knock . . ."

"He wouldn't be yours." Great-grandmother nodded. "But my dear girl, don't you see that you've already broken the chain? The chain that binds all of us and pounds at our doors?"

Camilla looked into her face. The things that face has experienced. But Camilla didn't see how she would hear the knock again.

"Liam. He's the first boy born to an Olsen woman in generations. You won the jackpot of luck, sweet girl." Gigi smiled. "Not only do you have a beautiful boy to raise up, but you have another knock coming. And I suggest you answer when it comes."

"What if I don't?"

My mother looked at me, her face not at all happy about our family reunion. "You will answer it, Camilla. You must."

Camilla considered what lay before her. Generations of her family represented around one dining table. Her mother ignored the knock and spent her life chasing dreams and stability. Her aunt answered it and built up an enviable career. Nana welcomed the knock and pushed through her difficulties to make a good life for herself and her daughters. Gigi.

"Gigi. Did you answer or ignore the knock?" Camilla asked.

Gigi smiled. "Ignored it, of course. Too busy on the farm. Had my girls with my Bill before he up and died on me. Raised my girls. Lost the farm. Answer the knock, darling girl. Make us proud."

Camilla woke up in her bed of overstuffed pillows and pile of quilts to the sound of Liam drumming in the next room. She rubbed her eyes and stumbled out of her warm cocoon towards the bedroom door. Camilla pulled on her robe. She pushed his door open to tease him about waking her up so early when she realized he was still asleep. Bum in the air, thumb in his mouth. Out cold.

Confused, Camilla walked down the short hallway to the kitchen. She heard the banging sound again. Except as her head cleared, she realized it wasn't a banging sound at all but a tapping at her front door. A persistent tapping.

Author Intro

HELENA PANEYKO

I am an interesting hybrid of nationalities and cultures. I have worn many hats over the years, all of them with passion and dedication.

I was born and raised in Venezuela, where I became a Veterinarian. I also had a radio talk show and weekly wrote for a national newspaper. I was the first woman President of the Student's Body and a Congress Representative, the youngest at that time.

I moved to the United States with my two children in 1997. I continued my education and went back to school, receiving a Master's Degree in Education. That led me to employment as a Spanish Professor at the Defense Language Institute, as an interpreter and a translator.

My curiosity and willingness to go back to Nature took me to Ireland, where I lived on an Organic Farm for a year. I walked El Camino de Santiago by myself, one of the most rewarding personal adventures . . . so far! Along the way, I have been writing. I have published two books of short stories and a poem that was included in the first *Rainshadow Poetry Anthology*. I am now a proud grandmother of two beautiful girls, Amelia and Ariana.

You can contact Helena at helenapaneyko@gmail.com or call 360-774-1513.

THE NAKED SNAKE

I woke before sunrise, taking advantage of the cool morning, which evaporates quickly these days. I went, with my loyal dog Mia, for our daily walk. She looked different as if she was sensing changes coming our way. I could not read the message in her eyes.

I usually enjoy the songs of the birds welcoming the new day, but now, adding to the canine's instinct, all was silent.

A long skinny black line seemed to be painted on the sidewalk, a sidewalk we have used every day and hadn't noticed the skinny black line before. Maybe it was a new kind of graffiti. Looking more closely I realized that the line was a line of dead ants, and not a painted one. Have they committed mass suicide?

While checking on them I felt as if something was falling from the sky. No, they were not cats and dogs, they were birds, fainting, hitting the ground, some of them dying, others unconscious.

Cockroaches belly up, geckos trying to hide under the rocks, naked snakes circling the evaporated lake that had hosted swimmers and kayakers just a few days prior. Everything seemed so unreal, so strange.

The trees looked as if they were on strike, sitting-down. The flowers, bent over looking at the ground, appeared exhausted.

Mia and I decided to turn around and head home. On our way back, and we had not gone that far, the asphalt looked as if it were smoking. The few passing cars started to swerve uncontrollably.

I sat in front of my computer. The keyboard gave the impression of dancing and the symbols, like in a soup of letters, were all out of control.

The air conditioner had stopped working.

The sun, already awake, seemed to be having fun with the new game it had invented. Or was it exercising revenge for all the damage we have done to our planet?

Clouds were moving away. They did not cry with rain, now they sweated.

I turned around to see the thermometer I have on the wall. It had exploded.

I wanted to drink some water. There was none.

My misted glasses impeded a clear view of my surroundings. My upper and lower eyelashes intertwined making my sight more difficult by the moment.

Everything looked dry. Everything was disappearing like the ashes from a mad volcano.

Night arrived, and the sun did not want to leave.

Then, I fainted. Mia was by my side.

THE INVISIBLE WRITER

I worked at a Post Office close to my home. I was assigned to a Special Department that was created to receive and catalog lost mail lacking an addressee. New letters arrived daily.

I read and classified them by my own intuition: there were those of love, those of pain, those of farewells, those of Christmases, those of hopes and despairs, those of welcoming.

The Christmas ones were kept in a big red box, decorated with motifs from those festivities. They were usually written by children, although I also found some with the handwriting of elderly people. Those of the children, with large and unequal letters, often came with drawings and sentences such as: "I know I have not behaved very well this year, but . . . " The elderly folks showed trembling hands, and they no longer asked for material things.

There were many letters of congratulations for birthdays, graduations, anniversaries, babies, new houses. I placed these in a blue box with divisions according to the occasion. Letters of grieving were filed in a separate box.

The love letters, the most numerous, were difficult to open and even to classify because I felt guilty about sniffing around in the lives of others. But I did it because they were all anonymous to me. Some were faraway sweethearts, others imaginary ones, all with uncertain endings. They would never reach their intended destinations.

As I have always been curious, I noticed that some of the letters had the same handwriting on very thin and soft paper. I created another classification for them. As I read through them, they made me laugh and made me cry. They made me suffer and made me dream.

Each of those letters was loaded with false illusions. I began to fall in love with the invisible writer, to visualize him without really knowing how he looked. I started collecting the letters without permission from my supervisor, and I took them home where I reread them again and again.

Years passed. But one day, another of these special letters arrived. This time it was sent to me.

It was a unique letter where my invisible writer, now my favorite, invited me to have coffee. The day and time were specified. It was at a café called Better Living Through Coffee I frequented in the afternoons after leaving my daily job. I almost had a heart attack when I read it. I began to tremble with emotion, but also with a little fear. Was I imagining everything or was it real?

The day of our date arrived, and I stood in front of the coffee shop holding his letter in my hand so he would recognize me.

He not only recognized me, but he already knew who I was.

When I saw him, I threw myself into his arms without thinking twice. It was the same face I had imagined, only now it had become real. From then on, the letters became words with sounds that came out of his lips accompanied by the music of his very distinct accent.

Dreams and illusions have their way of manifesting.

My dreams took years to manifest, but when they came true . . .

Author Intro

MARLENE LEWIS

My husband and I have recently retired to Sequim from Alaska, and we are immersing ourselves in many activities as well as the history and culture of this fascinating place and loving it all. Besides continuing to hike, camp, and paddle, I became certified as a Master Gardener from the WSU Clallam County Extension and volunteer for a variety of activities sponsored by the Master Gardeners. I'm also scraping the rust off my pen and writing.

A brief summary of my forty-six years in Alaska reveals my eclectic life, or, as some cynics may point out, my short attention span. Advanced degrees in English, History, and Education weren't necessarily required for many of the jobs I held, but they do come in handy for small talk at cocktail parties. Among the positions I found interesting in one way or another were commercial insurance underwriter, boarding stable owner, university instructor, retail display, secretary, budget analyst, birch syrup entrepreneur, and—as the attached essay indicates—a disciplined, motivated soldier.

Although I won't have another forty-six years on the Peninsula, I should have plenty of new experiences here that will find their way onto paper.

Marlene Lewis can be reached at marlene.shinn.lewis@gmail.com.

YOUR LEFT, YOUR RIGHT, YOUR LEFT...

I do solemnly swear that I will support and defend the
Constitution of the United States and of the State of
Alaska against all enemies, foreign and domestic; that I
will bear true faith and allegiance to the same; and that I
will obey the orders of the President of the United States
and the Governor of Alaska and the orders of the
officers appointed over me, according to regulations and
the Uniform Code of Military Justice. So help me God.

On September 26, 1979, I took this oath and signed my
name to a stack of forms acknowledging that I understood
what I was doing; that all my questions had been satisfactorily
answered; that my actions were voluntary; that I didn't do
drugs (except as prescribed by a licensed physician); that I
never intentionally sniffed hairspray; that I had no known
personality disorders; that I was heterosexual and proud of it;
that I was not known on a first-name basis by the FBI; and that
everything I had signed was true, true, true. If I ever run
across Army Recruiter Staff Sergeant Louie M. Albright again,
I will personally and gleefully do harm to his body, now that
I've learned how.

I can't really fault the military, at least not for my initial
decision to join. I was well into adulthood and successfully
climbing the junior executive ladder of a large insurance
company. I traveled, had a healthy expense account, came
and went as I wished, rubbed elbows with the right people. I
was bored. I was also restyling my life after my divorce from
a man who had once told me, among other things, that I could
not join the National Guard for a weekend job. I joined for all
the wrong reasons.

Louie Albright didn't intentionally lead me astray when I
talked to him about joining. He just hadn't caught up on the

last thirty-two directives and bulletins collecting in a wire basket on top of his file cabinet. So when he told me I could go through Basic Training right here in Alaska, he thought he was right. When he told me that females went through only two weeks of Basic Training, he thought he was right. And when he said I could be assigned to the unit of my choice with no problem, he thought he was right.

Louie Albright was right about one thing; I enlisted under a split option, which meant that I could start my weekend warrioring right away and defer my Basic Training for up to one year. However, when August 1980 rolled around, I found a few surprises waiting for me. One, I was too old to go to Basic Training without a waiver from Washington (which was quickly obtained). Two, Basic Training would be with the Regular Army for the standard eight weeks. Three, my Basic Training would be at Fort Leonard Wood, Missouri. Four, I had just enough time to tell my employer and my family and pick up my plane ticket.

We waited tensely in a detention center euphemistically called the Reception Station by the Army—mostly teenagers: long hair, beards, hip, punk, Northern, Southern, city street-wise, country bumpkin, defiant, intimidated, determined, unsure. The heat boiled up from the flat Missouri landscape. After stoically trying to adjust to the drastic change in weather from Alaska, I gracefully passed out on the second day from heat prostration. My fellow inmates carried me into the sergeant's cool office where I was revived. The sergeant was very big and very Southern. He yelled at me, he mocked me, he censured me, he yelled some more, and he kicked me out of his office.

"We want to welcome you to your temporary home here at Fort Leonard Wood." Thanks.

The first week went by in a blur. The males were shaved and looked identical for a while. We were "processed." Building after building, in one door and out another, collecting along the way fatigues, cotton underwear, dress uniforms, shoes, boots, hats, brass, dog tags, jackets, raincoats, helmets, ammo pouches, field belts, canteens, towels, bed linens, pillows, and a nifty duffle bag to carry all this in. My duffle bag weighed more than I did at the time, but I found hidden strength to carry it when one sergeant barked at me—I didn't like the alternative he offered.

We had shots and eye exams, learned how to brush our teeth ("self-applied fluoride treatment"), had more shots, met the chaplain, reviewed our contracts (did I really sign that?), had more shots. I don't remember much about the food at the Reception Station that first week except that there was always Jell-O and it was always melted. Our barracks that first week would have fascinated a student of 1940 military architecture as well as a professional pest control expert. There were only four of us females in a three-story, 96-bed building. After lights-out, it was positively eerie.

Camaraderie blossomed over a cozy, albeit mandatory, evening pastime—boot polishing. We quickly learned that the Army has a twisted sense of humor. There was never enough time before lights-out to work on our boots so they'd pass inspection the next morning, and we were forbidden to do anything after lights-out. Now that I look back on it, I guess the sergeants knew, but at the time we thought we were putting something over on them by polishing our boots by flashlight under the blankets or in the latrine by the thin sliver of light under the hallway door.

Suitably humble and properly attired, we left the Reception Station at the end of the first week to report to our respective Basic Combat Training companies. I was assigned to Bravo Company; two hundred twenty-eight of us were divided into five platoons, three male and two female. As we marched from the bus stop to our new barracks, it was drilled into us that of the five companies Bravo was always the best, and we screamed cadence at the top of our lungs to let the rest of the post know.

The next seven weeks were, bar none, the worst of my life. The only way I got through was by sheer determination to prove I could do it—to myself and to all the drill instructors who told me I couldn't.

During the next two weeks, we were not allowed to talk to each other. We weren't allowed phone calls or mail. We had no free time. The majority of the company was under 18, away from home for the first time, and giddy with so many of the Opposite Sex close by. So our two weeks of silence, because it hadn't been, stretched into three and a half. I would have gladly throttled every Barbie Doll in my platoon to keep them quiet, but the paperwork afterward would have been a bother.

Our time was spent alternating from classroom instruction to PT to drill-and-ceremony to field training. We moaned out of bed each morning at 4:30 and were in formation by 4:45. Don't tell me a female can't get up, make the bed, wash, dress, brush teeth, do hair, and be on time for an appointment in fifteen minutes. We did it. Thanks to many vivid reminders from the drill instructors of the consequences of not doing it.

After formation every morning, the company marched together through the darkness to the PT field. We stripped down to T-shirts and spent an agonizing thirty minutes doing things to our bodies that were cruel punishments. Even more stressing were the drill sergeants, walking among us like angels of death, singling out for ridicule those who couldn't keep up. I found out that since it was pretty dark anyway, I could get by with bending a lot, flapping my arms, and groaning. To ensure that we worked up an appetite for chow, we then ran in formation for two or three miles. I found it hard at first to sing cadence while gasping desperately for air, but gradually I got the hang of it—and the beat too: "C-130 GOIN' DOWN THE STRIP, AIRBORNE MAMA GONNA TAKE A LITTLE TRIP . . . "

The high points of each day were chow. I've never eaten so much for so long in my life. Unfortunately, chow didn't delay the next round of activities scheduled for us. The classroom sessions were deadly. The Missouri heat, coupled with the crowded rooms, created cozy incubators ideal for snoozing. The drill sergeants didn't see it that way. Offenders had to stand; even then some fell asleep on their feet. We always tried surreptitiously to pinch a fellow trainee awake before the sergeants grabbed him, but they were usually too quick for us.

We learned that each one of us would soon emerge from Basic Training as a "disciplined, motivated soldier who is qualified with his basic weapon, physically conditioned and drilled in the fundamentals of soldiering." We saw films, we heard lectures, we had demonstrations of all aspects of military custom and courtesy. We learned how and when to salute, sit, stand, talk. We learned about the Uniform Code of Military Justice—over and over and over. The UCMJ was tattooed on our minds, and we knew all of the ways to get court martialed.

We spent only one day on first aid, first the theory then the real thing—fumbling with each other's arms and legs.

CPR, fortunately, was practiced on a dummy. In the Modern Army you are allowed only to stop breathing, go into shock, or wound an arm or leg.

Gas mask drill was kind of exciting. The sergeants didn't spring it on us; they let us have all day to look forward to it. As we went through in groups of nine or ten, we found out what stuff we were made of. We filed into the chamber with our gas masks on and watched with curiosity as the gas filled the little room. Then over the loud speaker the sergeant ordered us to take our masks off. The longer anyone in the group hesitated, the longer we had to stand in the gas without protection. Those of us who left the chamber coughing and choking passed. Throwing up didn't count. Only three out of the whole company ran out screaming and sobbing hysterically.

The main attraction at Fort Leonard Wood is weapons training. After a brief engagement, we were formally married to our M-16's; we zeroed our own, cleaned them, repaired them, fired them, cleaned them again, protected them, and sometimes even slept with them. It is a deceptively simple weapon designed for incredibly simple destruction. I could break mine down completely and have it back together, loaded and ready to fire again, in three-and-a-half minutes. The M-16 is a semi-automatic weapon. The fully automatic M-60 is its grown-up cousin, a little more complicated to break down and clean, not as portable, but a dandy weapon for single-handedly wiping out a small town. Since they tend to bounce around a bit, we fired the M-60's in pairs from a prone position. Daytime firing was impressive enough. However, the night we went to the range to fire the M-60's, it was Fourth of July all over again. We loaded tracer bullets that left a blazing trail all the way to the target. I had so much fun watching the fireworks down the firing range that I didn't even bother aiming for the targets. I don't think the sergeants cared. We were never tested on night firing; I figured that so far we were training only for the U.S. Army Daytime Division.

The LAW, light anti-tank weapon, is an interesting gadget. It looks like a hollow plastic tube about three inches in diameter and three feet long when extended. It weighs several ounces, fits nicely on the shoulder, has no recoil whatsoever, and will take out a tank in one hit. Our target tank was already dead, but we got the idea of the power behind that gentle "whoosh." The backblast of the LAW, the air that explodes out the back of the tube, is powerful enough to kill a person up to 40 feet away. The sergeants were very careful that day.

We spent lots of time practicing our grenade throwing with heavy round metal duds. Poised like a ballet dancer on the battlefield, I'd assume a graceful stance, yell some directions, point like a retriever, and let loose with the grenade. All according to instructions. I never did understand why we were supposed to give the enemy so much time to see where we were going to throw the grenade. Due to military spending cutbacks, trainees were allowed only one live grenade to throw. This was the only time I ever saw the drill sergeants nervous.

I felt pretty confident when I walked up to the concrete bunker, actually just a three-sided wall about as high as my armpits. My steel pot never did fit very well, and it kept slipping over my forehead as First Sergeant Wells carefully lectured me about live grenades. I wasn't worried because I knew I could throw fairly well for a female, and a live grenade would be even more incentive to hurl it far away. Sergeant Wells stood to one side of the bunker; I stood in it and prepared my elaborate *ballet d'grenade*. Only this time I had a real pin to pull. I was elated. I pulled the pin, drew my arm slowly back, and made a perfectly timed throw. The wall of the bunker got in my way. My hand smashed into the concrete, and the grenade rolled out of my fist onto the ground directly in front of the bunker. Sergeant Wells was close to retiring, but not that close. I never saw him move so fast, before or after. He leapt the wall in a single bound and flattened me to the ground as the grenade exploded. I didn't care for the look on his face when I asked if I could have another chance.

The nice thing about Basic Training is that if you're not particularly good at one thing, there's plenty more to try. So I forgot the grenade incident and went on to shine in Riot Control. There were about thirty of us National Guardsmen, and we were pulled out of the company occasionally for special NG training. These sessions were almost enjoyable since there were fewer of us and the sergeant who accompanied us was always more relaxed and friendly. Probably because the Guardsmen didn't use weapons that go bang.

We spent two days on Riot Control. Once I found out that it was OK to be as aggressive as I wanted toward last term's trainees who played our adversaries, I was in National Guard heaven. I learned to use a riot stick both as an offensive weapon and for defense. I learned how to control crowds, quell riots, round up looters and snipers, and how to growl. I was a good growler. I took my growling seriously. My *coup de grace* came when I really did scare one of my adversaries. He looked shocked at first, then retreated in confusion. I was jubilant. I'd found my niche.

And I was ready for Louie Albright.

Author Intro

RUTH GEIGER

I write poetry and reflective prose. I've had a variety of life experiences: participating in an archaeological dig in Israel, internship in a New Zealand church, parenting eight boys in a Children's home in Cleveland, and working with abused children. I was a correspondence teacher for special needs children in Alaska for 20 years, and a United Methodist pastor in Alaska and Seattle for 17 years.

I write about growing up in an alcoholic home, life as a hippie, challenging experiences as a single parent of five adopted children — four from Haiti, and one from Philadelphia. Each of these children has special needs: a wannabe gang member, one mentally ill, one who suffered physical and sexual abuse, one in detention for two years, and my two sons who I sent to an emotional growth school in Mexico. I write about the experience of a black child with a white mom.

I live in Sequim Washington with my wife Brenda, two cats, a Golden Retriever, and five noisy chickens. I like to travel, garden, write, and be with my five grandchildren. I love retirement! I am writing a book called *When Love Isn't Enough*.

Ruth can be reached at ruthgeiger@olypen.com

WE FORGOT THE TENT POLES

Camping on the Olympic Peninsula was one of my children's favorite summer activities when they were younger. As a single parent of five adopted children, it was a special time that I could afford.

Everyone had a gathering task to accomplish before we could leave home.

Necessities
Sleeping bags?   ✓
Pillows?   ✓
Tent ?   ✓
Clothes?   ✓
Toys?   ✓
Matches?   ✓

Utensils
Silverware?   ✓
Pots and Pans?   ✓

Food and Drink
Snacks?   ✓
Water?   ✓
Drinks?   ✓
Hot dogs?   ✓
Buns?   ✓
Ketchup, Mustard? ✓
S'more fixings?   ✓
Fruit?   ✓

List complete. The van was loaded to the max with little room for passengers. It was a good thing I had a large Dodge Caravan.

"Do we have everything?"

We thought so. I waited in the house while my children bickered over who would ride shotgun. Once that was decided, I got in the car, and we headed for Lake Crescent. Lots of enthusiastic anticipation to go camping. No enthusiasm for the car ride. It didn't take long before the youngest child said she had to go to the bathroom. The middle child complained too, "I'm hungry." The oldest child didn't care much since she was busy talking on her cell phone. The oldest boy wanted to know when would we get there.

Fortunately, the campground was only two hours away. After we arrived, we all piled out of the van at the same time. The older children wanted to go explore. First things first. The first thing on my list was to set up the tent. It was a rather large tent. Large enough for my two sons to be on one side, my oldest daughter in the other section, and the two and three year olds in the middle section with me.

We put down the tarp and carefully placed the tent on top of it. There were always rocks in the way, but we were able to pound in the corner pegs. Next the tent poles.

"Mike, please go get the tent poles."

He returned shortly. "Mom, they aren't there."

"What do you mean they are not there? Cathy, you go look for the tent poles."

She returned quickly. "Everything is out of the van, and there are no tent poles."

"Who was supposed to put the tent poles in the car?"

Of course, no one took responsibility. Now what?

The middle child started to cry. "Do we have to go back home and get the poles?"

It was already 4 pm, and I was tired of driving. The kids were tired of riding. The thought of getting in a car with five hungry, tired children did not appeal to me. The thought of sleeping in the van with five kids didn't appeal either. It was a clear night, and only a few gentle clouds were drifting by. There was no rain in the forecast. We decided to sleep under the stars. The younger girls were afraid there might be bugs. The older boys hoped there would be bugs so they could torment their sisters.

After swimming, we hung our wet towels on a rope between the trees which marked off our camping spot. We took turns roasting hot dogs. The s'mores were messy as expected, but delicious.

We laid out our sleeping bags on top of the tarps. The coolness of the night didn't invade the warmth of our down sleeping bags, and we were very cozy. Darkness began to show over the tree tops. At 10 pm the sun light gradually left behind its layer of multiple shades of pink as it disappeared over the horizon, marking the end of another day. If we had been inside our tent, we would have missed that beautiful sunset. My children fell asleep to the sound of a frog croaking for a mate. For a brief moment it was quiet.

About 5:30 am the birds commenced their morning calls. It didn't take long until the other animals awakened with my children. We couldn't believe that we spent the whole night outside and weren't bothered by little critters or a deer looking for something to nibble.

Without the tent poles we experienced things we never would have seen or felt inside a tent. The wind gently blowing across our faces, the silence of the sunset; the call of an owl. What started as a disaster became a happy camping memory. Even if we did forget the tent poles.

OUR FRIENDSHIP

We have been to this place before.
Do you remember?
My daughter and her friend played in the sand.
We pretended to eat their seaweed pies.
The ones they made for us.
It was a perfect day
Hot, but not too hot
Cool, but not too cool.
We sat on a log and talked while the children played.
I don't remember what we talked about.
I do remember
Another special day in our friendship.

I LEARNED

I learned to ignore

· my mother's mandates
· loud TV commercials
· the humming of the refrigerator
· the washer spinning

I learned to ignore

· pan handlers
· world news
· children crying
· the voice of God

I learned to listen for

· water boiling
· a microwave's ding
· a cell phone's song
· the ice cream truck

I learned to listen for

· words unspoken
· silence between gentle waves
· birds chirping a wake-up call
· the voice of God

AN ALOE PLANT

We have an aloe plant at our house.
You can break off a piece, open it, and squeeze out the juice.
The liquid will heal your outer wounds.
We have no plant to heal our inner wounds.
Often that takes much longer.
Those wounds aren't always visible.
Not to others.
Sometimes not even to ourselves.

Author Intro

JUDITH R. DUNCAN

Writing stories and poems helps me understand myself. Through writing I discover what I think about self-determination, life after death, and how to live a fulfilling life. Many of my stories are based on the lives of neighbors, family, and farm life in rural Missouri where I lived for eighteen years.

Growing up on a dairy farm in the foothills of the Ozarks, my primary childhood responsibility was tending the chickens: feeding, watering, gathering eggs and helping to butcher them. Often my poems are told through the characters of the chickens that I raised–their quarrels and troubles.

Nature is another theme of my writing. As a youngster, I wandered through oak-hickory forests surrounding our farm to observe and enjoy trees, flowers and wildlife. Today, I believe that a walk in the woods solves almost everything that worries me.

Last week my husband and I returned from hiking in the Canadian Rockies where we both fell in love with the sense of isolation and peace we felt on the Lake Helen Trail. Upon our return to Sequim one of my first chores was to bury Butthead, my oldest and smallest chicken. I will surely be writing a poem about the Canadian mountains and little Butthead.

Judy can be contacted at PO Box 171, Carlsborg, WA 98324

SIX WOMEN DELIBERATE AT THE CLALLAM COUNTY COURTHOUSE

I adore the bailiff

she adores the bailiff

we all adore the bailiff

this scrumptious officer of the court.

His straight-backed authority

the weapon on his hip

tight butt in his khakis –

a beacon on a treacherous shore

overcome by heat I swim nude in his blue eyes.

Stop. Ladies, get a grip!

We deliberate – how to entice him

to the bar across the street

for pool, dancing and beer.

THE VERDICT

Who is not guilty of transgression?
Who is not tempted to break a window
yell drunkenly on the sidewalk beneath
the balcony of a loved one who's
kissing someone else tonight.

We each have a rock of mischief
hidden knotted anger
a crazy do-wop-wop in our heart
a need for revenge and relief.

In the courtroom, hold your head high
scrub clean of sin, wear a clean shirt
hold a stiff posture next to your shaggy-headed
saggy-panted public defender.

Guilty-guilty-guilty
jurors #3 and #4
the man in the third row of the gallery
prosecuting attorney, the black robed judge
all guilty of envy, jealousy, and coveting
the butt of the bailiff.

WALK IN THE WOODS

I've been snailed, huckleberried
unfurled & seeped
in a bog of skunk cabbage–
slickened & all mossed-up.
The best I've smelled in years!

INTO THE WOODS

I take to the woods
note every yellow, slick gray slug
dendritic veins of fallen leaves
trails of worm casings
crumbly hills of voles
owl droppings.
Black and brown woolies
the green moss-cushion
upon which I tread
upturned, overturned
earth treasures
gifts of the ground.
I pleasure at what I see at my feet
filled with softness, I walk home.

CIRCLING THE EDGES

of water-soaked soils

stepping lightly

around tired ground.

Watching daily the muck dry

through April, to pliable clods by May.

April sun nourishes early peas

a full dash of summer heat

grows green beans–

ripens autumn pears.

Huge abundance deepens

the roots of our love.

Poetry Corners 2018, Arts & Humanities Bainbridge

CEDAR WAXWINGS

Before sunrise raiders in black masks

drawn to the scent of purple –

filch the fruit of the Juneberry.

A flock of eight descend

thrash the tree top, sway twigs

shutter leaves, pilfer berries.

Not yet sunlight

they swarm in silence

no high pitch scree-scree

no flash of bronze-green feathers

yellow painted tail, nor scarlet wing dot.

Gone, jam for scones

syrup for pancakes

gone to the predawn raiders

gone to the belly of the bird.

Tidepools 2018

MY SIX HENS

know who they are

where they are going–

except for the road thing.

With confidence & puffed feather dignity

they lounge in cedar shavings

eat organic corn.

A life replete with Buddhist calm

Wi-Fi music

winter heat lamps.

Yet, when I gaze into Polly's eyes

I see grief–

existential grief.

NEW RULES

This is dangerous ground for us.

You on the verge of retirement.

I clutch privacy

to my breast like a lover–

protective and indecent.

Whom do I love?

The you who lives across the Bay or

the you in my kitchen disturbing my spoons.

Poetry Corners 2017. Arts & Humanities Bainbridge

WATCHING THE SUN CREEP

across the carpet toward the sleeping hound

deer follow their path single file to the river

hens quarrel in the coop over remains of corn

drinking another cup of coffee

watching the wind bow the willows

shadows lengthen, a fly dies at the window sill

sitting in this chair, motives are classified

hidden from those who care

I delay moving from morning into afternoon

a missed airplane through future time zones

no-show to an intimate dinner

failure to see life's parade

passing me by is of no consequence

THE ONLY SONGBIRD THAT SWIMS

In a dark pocket of damp
soft mossy green
a gray feathered
American Dipper sings.

Dark eyes with pale lids
focus on floating larva.
She dives into the Hoh
feeds on dragonfly nymphs
dives deeper for tadpoles.

Beneath a rocky overhang
a nest-dome of sedges
side door facing south
hides three nestlings
peeping open beaks.

Green with dot of yellow
a Dolly Varden trout
peach-blushed belly
a sinuous ribbon
wide open mouth

doesn't plan to eat a bird
whose swift movement
underwater dances
rhythmic flirtation
is mistaken for a water bug.

It's rare that a fish eats a bird
not a common peril
for a lady Dipper
mother of three.

Tidepools 2016

HOW CHICKENS LOST THEIR TEETH AND GOT THEIR BEAKS

101 million years ago, or so
the velociraptor
a ferocious land raptor
of large teeth and muscular jaw

evolved to Ichthyosaurus
with the aspect of a tern
beak
teeth
feathers

behold
this missing link
flying above the Kansan sea
dinosaurian toothed jaw
diving
crunching
feasting on crabs

haunting Polly Chicken
swimming in her eyes
lost ancestral days
brimming in her brain
ripping
tearing
seafood flesh
longing for her teeth

Author Intro

MARILYN J. NELSEN

My husband and I moved to Sequim in 2007 after a year-long odyssey, traveling across the country in an RV from North Carolina to the Pacific Northwest. In many ways this was a homecoming for me. As a native Washingtonian, I spent most of my life in California where I received my education, raised a family, and worked for over forty years. I was drawn to working with older adults from an early age, and served as a social services provider, community educator, and family therapist. After moving back to Washington, I worked for several years with a local hospice organization here on the Olympic Peninsula.

I describe myself as a life-long learner, having returned to school once a decade throughout my adult life. My undergraduate degree in English Lit suggests my deep love of literature and the craft of writing. I hold a Master's degree in counseling and a doctorate in depth psychology. I recently completed my first novel and am currently working on edits. My short story, *Flying Lessons,* has been a labor of love, as it touches on themes of aging and the life of a spunky senior who refuses to let age and circumstances define her.

Marilyn's new cozy mystery *Writing Can Be Murder* will be available fall 2018 on Amazon.com. Details on her release schedule will appear at bookmarksnbroomsticks.blogspot.com.

FLYING LESSONS

I was quite old when I learned to fly – eighty-two or eighty-three, as I recall. Numbers and dates tend to get muddled these days, so I really can't be certain. I do remember feeling curious about my approaching death around this same time, though. Death is an ever-present reality in your eighties, and all around me people were saying their final good-byes, leaving great gaping holes in my life. Reading the obituaries was no longer an interesting diversion, but an obligation marked by a mixture of morbid curiosity and dread.

Looking back, I know that flying was the last thing on my mind that drab Seattle afternoon. Although it was early spring, the Emerald City wasn't very emerald and tempers were flaring in response to our long confinement. A relentless downpour had kept us residents prisoners in our cell-like rooms, except for mealtime. Like dutiful automatons, we marched to the dining room three times a day – breakfast, lunch and dinner. I had finally rebelled, huffing and puffing my discontent with the dreary world and my even drearier existence. *Independent living, my scrawny ass!* I had stormed to no one in particular.

Donning my rain gear, I stepped onto the balcony of my second story apartment, daring the elements to stop me. As I stood there staring discontentedly at my water-logged plants and what appeared to be the only healthy specimen left (a magnificent fern that kept resurrecting itself year after year), the sun made a belated appearance, breaking through the banks of clouds that were gradually drifting apart like . . . I wracked my brain for a suitable simile, tantalized by the memory of a line from a raunchy detective story I'd been secretly reading. And then it came back to me: "clouds drifting apart *like exhausted lovers.*" My satisfaction with this small feat of memory was short-lived, though.

Feeling increasingly disgruntled, I stood there debating what action to take. Just as I was preparing to go back inside, a rainbow materialized in the distance stretching across the sky. Its southernmost leg disappeared behind Saint Barnabas Episcopal Church just as the ancient steeple bells began to chime, an anomaly that left me feeling disoriented and a bit wobbly on my feet. Then, as if to emphasize this odd coincidence, I found myself lifted up, as if on angels' wings, floating a few inches above the balcony floor. I hovered there for a few tantalizing moments before settling back on the concrete surface with a jolt, just as the church bells stopped ringing.

My first reaction was to wonder if I had imagined the whole thing, but before I could fully assimilate what had happened, reality returned with a trickle of icy water down the back of my neck. Reaching around, I found that the brim of my rain hat had come down in the back, releasing a rivulet of trapped water. Rubbing my neck with one gloved hand, I stared up at the place where I had seen the rainbow. It was no longer there. Not believing my eyes, I looked again. Could it possibly have disappeared so quickly . . . so completely?

Oh fine, I thought, one more sign of encroaching senility. Now I was hallucinating. I peeked over my shoulder to see if anyone was watching. One never knew when Vera might show up to monitor my medication or snoop through my dresser to see if I was hiding cookies or other forbidden contraband. My recent diagnosis of type 2 diabetes meant that anything sweet was strictly forbidden, and Vera was nothing if not vigilant in protecting me from any possibility of self-sabotage.

Vera, aka "Snoop-Face" (my secret name for her, and a completely ineffectual way of expressing my rebellion over being spied upon), had been my son Andy's idea. Just one more way of keeping me from experiencing anything remotely associated with pleasure. Vera was a personal caregiver, an independent contractor who worked through the facility, hired by concerned families to assist residents with their daily care.

Once I had determined that Snoop-Face wasn't anywhere near, I turned my attention back to the now rapidly darkening sky, searching my memory for anything that might help to explain this strange experience with the rainbow. I wondered rather distractedly why I hadn't heard the dinner bell announcing the nightly cattle call to the dining room. Perhaps the church bells had blocked out the sound. *Strange, though, because this had never happened before.*

Tipping my head back once again, I peered up at the sky feeling the same sense of disorientation I had felt earlier. I wondered briefly if I might be having a TIA (those mini-strokes we older folks sometimes have) and debated whether I should call for help. Yet I continued standing there, riveted to the spot. Perhaps the thought of being taken to the hospital was sufficiently sobering. In my experience, hospitals were places you went to die, and I wasn't quite ready to make that trip yet.

Darkness was rapidly approaching by this time (*where had the afternoon gone?*), and I was becoming increasingly aware of how strange it was that Vera hadn't come to escort me to dinner. Actually, everything was feeling slightly off-kilter. I was aware of not being in the least bit hungry, despite a light lunch and no afternoon snack.

Ignoring my fleeting concern about a possible TIA and lack of appetite, I decided to take advantage of those few rare moments of freedom. Stars were beginning to appear in the night sky, which suggested that the rain had finally moved on. I pulled my coat closer against the cool evening air, tightening the belt around my waist – the fleece lining felt warm and comforting against my skin.

As I stood there staring up at the stars, I became aware of a tingling sensation rippling through my body, something I hadn't felt in years: the sensation of being totally and completely *alive!* Perhaps it was the break in my usual routine, coupled with the heady sense of doing something forbidden – like a child playing hooky from school. Whatever the reason, it was glorious. I drew closer to the balcony railing, grasping it with both hands, pulling myself up on tiptoes to feel closer to the stars. I longed for that sense of freedom that had accompanied my earlier sensation of floating above the balcony. For a brief moment, I found myself lifted up once again, hovering above the balcony floor. Suddenly I was soaring up, up, up into the sky, completely and totally free of all earthly ties. It must have been only a moment or two before it was over, but it was more real than anything I had felt in a long time. Millions and millions of stars swirling around me and colors too vivid to describe, a kaleidoscope of endlessly expanding movement and space.

As I settled back down to earth, I found myself transported back to my childhood to one magical day on our farm in Minnesota when I had seen my first rainbow. I was around four at the time. I remember sitting on the ground spellbound, midway between the house and the barn, staring at a rainbow. It stretched across the sky following a brief electrical storm that knocked out power to the farm's chicken hatchery. Everyone was scurrying around frantically, ignoring me completely. My brother Jake almost tripped over me in his rush to help Papa.

"Geez, Midge, could you get out of the way before someone kills themselves tripping over you?" he grumbled, rubbing his shin. Midge was Jake's nickname for me, short for Midget, which wasn't really my name either. Christened Meredith at birth, I'd become Midget to my older brother when he was first introduced to me. Somewhat later, I became Midge, probably when he first saw me as an actual human being, worthy of a real name.

"Go in the house, why don't you," Jake admonished over his shoulder, not unkindly. "Mom's making lemonade and you can help her." He was off on a run again. He hadn't even noticed the rainbow. Already feeling the responsibility of the farm resting heavily on his eleven-year-old shoulders, he helped Papa with the chores and did odd jobs for Mama.

I didn't go into the house as directed, but stayed where I was, trying to look as inconspicuous as possible. I sat on the ground in my freshly laundered overalls, unaware of the dampness beneath me, legs tucked under me, hugging myself with skinny arms. In all the years afterward, I never got much beyond skinny.

This first encounter with a rainbow affected me profoundly, beckoning me with its dazzling colors and form. I remember wishing I could reach out and touch those brilliant colors that seemed to vibrate in the hot air all around me, air that was still charged with static electricity. It was my first conscious awareness of the mysteries of the natural world. Up until then, nature had been little more than a backdrop to the daily hustle and hardship of farm life.

As I wrapped myself in these memories, I recalled the World War II fighter pilot whose words touched me so deeply. Eighteen-year-old John Gillespie Magee, Jr., an American pilot with the Royal Canadian Air Force during WWII, had gone to Britain to fly in a Spitfire Squadron. He had written the poem "High Flight" at 30,000 feet during a test flight for a new model of the Spitfire V. Moved by his words, I'd committed portions of the poem to memory. It began, *"Oh, I have slipped the surly bonds of earth, And danced the skies on laughter-silvered wing,"* and ended *"with silent, lifting mind I've trod the high untrespassed sanctity of space, put out my hand and touched the face of God."*

Looking back now, I see how my four-year-old self might have resonated with Magee's epiphany, if only in embryonic form. I sat there on the ground contemplating the rainbow, reaching out in my imagination to touch each color in wonder and awe. I remained where I was, staring at the rainbow until it disappeared, and then stayed even longer hoping it would magically return. It wasn't until Mama called me into the house for dinner that I finally moved. It had been an overwhelming experience and I hadn't wanted it to end, nor had I wanted to share it with anyone in the family fearing they would make fun of me. Our family's no-nonsense approach to farm life didn't leave much room for imagination or sudden flights of fancy.

However, I'm getting away from my story, which is why I'm writing this account of those days when I first learned to fly.

The night after my adventure with the rainbow I slept soundly, not waking until Snoop-Face came in to rouse me. This in itself was unusual as I generally woke up several times during the night needing to pee. Vera seemed especially cheerful that morning and said nothing about my non-appearance at dinner the previous evening. Had I dreamed it all, I wondered, as I submitted to my morning ablutions? It was irritating not being allowed to wash and dress myself. I was perfectly capable of wielding a wash cloth and putting on my slacks and sweaters without help, but Vera felt it her duty to assist as that was part of what she was paid to do, so I played along with varying degrees of cooperation and contrariness. When I'm honest with myself, I imagine I was as much of a pain to her as she was to me.

When we were done swapping mutual grievances, Vera escorted me to the dining room where I joined the regulars at our table, hoping for, but equally certain that there wouldn't be any stimulating conversation. Henry had dementia and kept repeating himself which was tiring, but I didn't much care for the way the others kept reminding him that he'd told that same story over and over again. Sonia told us about her upcoming trip to Diamond Lake with her singularly boring family, the same trip they'd been taking every few months for as long as I could remember. I couldn't help wishing I was at another table, not that any of the other tables would have been an improvement. I finished my breakfast as quickly as possible and hurried back to my room.

Once inside, I looked at the room's newly restored tidiness. Housekeeping had made its invisible presence known: bed made, bathroom restored to its previous pristine order. Feeling irritated by the room's sterile oppressiveness, I tossed the neatly arranged throw pillows into a jumble of disorder on the couch, then scattered magazines across the coffee table, wishing I had some crumbs to spread on its polished surface. Having vented some of my frustration, I looked around for other diversions. Daytime TV bored me, and I'd finished my latest book of crossword puzzles.

I eased my body onto the sofa and tried to quiet my thoughts. Sensing the futility of my dissatisfaction, I let my mind drift back to the events of the previous evening. Once again, I found myself questioning my experiences. An old woman hallucinating, perhaps? The experience had certainly felt real at the time . . . more real than anything else in my humdrum life. But that didn't make it so, and there was no use pretending otherwise. Fighting a sense of deepening depression, I found myself staring out the window and tried to cheer myself with the thought that the weather had changed for the better. Sunlight was streaming through the sliding glass door that led onto the balcony, suggesting that spring had finally arrived. While I let myself dwell on that possibility, Snoop-Face came in to dispense my morning meds. I took them obediently, not feeling up to any further clashes with her.

"So do you have any plans for today?" she asked, an innocent expression on her face. If there was one thing I knew for certain it was that Snoop-Face was never innocent. She clearly had something up her sleeve. While I was forming a response, she began straightening the throw pillows and restacking the magazines. Fortunately, she didn't ask me why they were in disarray.

"Were you expecting me to have plans?" I asked, trying to look equally innocent. "Am I forgetting something important?"

"There's going to be a movie in the activities' room this afternoon with ice cream sundaes afterward. You'd enjoy that, wouldn't you?" she said, a new note of wheedling in her voice.

Ahh . . . the hook! Angie our Activity Director had obviously been talking with her. Not that I blamed Angie. She was a nice enough girl whose job came with a mandate to produce as many bodies as possible at each of her daily programs. She was too young of course to truly understand the wants and needs of seniors, but, then, how much can you really do that's novel and different with people whose mental and physical faculties are in decline, and whose families stay away for longer and longer periods of time between visits.

"I'll think about going," I lied. *Anything to get Snoop-Face out of my room.* She told me she'd be back to take me to lunch, and with a suspicious look left me to my own devices, but not before picking up the TV remote and flipping it on as she left. A game show host's raucous voice competed with the sound of drum rolls and audience applause. I hurried to turn it off. As I turned back to the couch, my attention was caught by the display of family photos on the wall that had become so familiar that I barely noticed them most of the time. Many were of family long gone, including my husband Frank who'd been with me for nearly sixty years before his death. I found myself staring at the picture of my brother Jake, forever enshrined in his U.S. Army Air Forces uniform, looking young and vulnerable.

Once again I felt the pull of the past and surrendered to memories of those days back on the farm, and to my brother Jake who had turned eighteen on the first day of December 1941, six days before Pearl Harbor was bombed. He'd enlisted immediately, training to be a fighter pilot just like John Gillespie Magee. I've often wondered if he had shared Magee's sense of the numinous while soaring high above the clouds. I would never know, as he like Magee had been killed the first year after enlisting. Both had been nineteen at the time of their death.

I stood there, feeling numb with remembrance. Shaking my head to clear these memories, I shifted my attention to the picture of my son Andy and his wife Kathleen, with their only son Jeremy by their side.

I was still standing there staring at the picture when I heard a soft knock on the door. I knew with certainty who was there. A mere coincidence? ESP? It really didn't matter; I simply knew. My grandson Jeremy (now in his early thirties) had promised to visit me soon the last time we'd talked. He'd given me an iPhone and taught me how to use it so we could text and FaceTime together. Jeremy's work schedule didn't allow him much free time, as he was employed twenty-five hours a week at a graphics design firm, and spent the remainder of his time promoting his art in galleries and other venues throughout Western Washington.

I opened the door to find Jeremy's smiling eyes staring at me above a bouquet of roses, carnations and baby's breath, my favorite flowers. His tall, lanky frame and easy grace always reminded me of Jake.

"Hi Grams," Jeremy said, extending the bouquet to me. "Hope I'm not interrupting your day. I was in town for a business meeting, and my schedule changed unexpectedly. Rather than calling you, I just jumped in the car and came over before anything else could get in the way."

Jeremy lived on the Olympic Peninsula in Port Townsend, so I wondered how he'd made it to the City so quickly, but before I could ask, he was already explaining the circumstances while giving me a big one-armed hug to avoid crushing the flowers. "I was supposed to meet with the owners of The Artists' Hole to finalize plans for showcasing my artwork in their bistro this summer, but they had a family crisis and had to reschedule for tomorrow morning. Are you free for a day on the town?"

"Free?" I said, dumbly, while digging out a vase from beneath the sink in my miniature kitchenette. "Yes, of course I am, unless you'd rather see an old movie in the activity room and have ice cream sundaes afterwards." I wasn't serious of course. Fortunately Jeremy, who's an unusually intuitive man, picked up on this fact. He gave me a sideways glance, as if to say, "Only if you twist my arm," and I quickly added, "but I'd much rather go out with you!"

"Good. We'll have lunch at a great little Italian place I found the last time I was in the City. Grab your coat and let's go have some fun."

Jeremy didn't have to tell me twice. I made a quick call to the office and left a message for Vera. Glancing outside one more time, I grabbed my lavender car coat from the closet (a nod to spring) and pulled on my purple beret with an amethyst broach pinned to its side.

"You look very fetching, Grams," Jeremy said, a twinkle in his eyes. The word *fetching* should have sounded odd coming from someone of his generation, but it somehow fit his old-soul persona.

The restaurant was as charming as Jeremy had said, and the proprietor acted as if we were regulars who were deserving of special attention. He seated us at a table beside a tile mural of Tuscan sunflowers, across from a small fountain that gurgled pleasantly in the background. We ordered wine (a rare treat for me), and after the antipasto, the chef came out and made pasta Alfredo tableside just like they'd done years ago when Frank and I had taken a Caribbean cruise on an Italian liner. I ate more than usual, marveling at how little guilt I felt while consuming a buttery pastry layered with creamy filling and topped with confectioner's sugar, something definitely verboten on my current dietary plan. I mentally gave old Snoop-Face a one-finger salute as I scraped the last crumbs off my plate. Clearly, Andy hadn't said anything to Jeremy about my recent diagnosis, and I thanked the fates. An occasional indulgence wasn't going to kill me.

As we sat over coffee, Jeremy shared his latest skirmish with his father. I knew from personal experience how incredibly insensitive Andy could be, and prepared myself to be irritated anew. Although Jeremy managed to make his recounting of their meeting somewhat humorous, I could detect the underlying hurt in his voice. The recent encounter was a recapitulation of an old argument between them, one that had never been resolved. It involved what Andy euphemistically called Jeremy's *lifestyle*. Jeremy was gay, something I'd known intuitively from his earliest years, long before he had acknowledged it to himself. We had formed a special bond from the beginning, and there was nothing that would ever change the love I felt for him. I listened with equal amounts of sympathy and exasperation: sympathy for Jeremy, exasperation for Andy, as he described the latest example of Andy's ongoing attempts to change his son.

"He'll never get it, you know," I said. "It's simply not in his DNA to identify with anyone who doesn't share his values and definition of what it means to be a man. But I really can't believe that he means to hurt you, Jeremy." I was feeling more generous towards Andy than usual, probably the result of the wine I'd consumed. "Anyway, I'm so sorry."

"Thanks, Grams. I didn't mean to spoil our luncheon with this stuff. It's just when you asked me how things had been going with dad, I couldn't bring myself to lie to you. I agree that the old guy isn't all that bad … he really can't wrap his head around the fact that my lifestyle isn't a reflection on him. As you say, he just doesn't get it."

"You know your father lives in fear of losing control," I commented, accepting it as fact. "It's an obsession with him. But the reality is that none of us is ever in control. It's just an illusion, this being in control thing."

Jeremy looked at me for a moment, softness in his eyes. "I love you, Grams," he said. "I'm so sorry I haven't been able to see you more often. It's tough getting a business up and running these days, especially when you're in the arts. But it's coming around now, and when I finally make it, you're going to come live with me." He studied me quietly. "I mean that," he said, "those aren't just words."

"I know you mean it," I said, "and it makes all the difference to me, whether it actually happens or not. At my age, one never knows."

"Don't say that, Grams . . . you'll never get old. I've always thought you were ageless." Jeremy smiled at me. "I bet you were a wonderful teacher . . . wish I'd had you when I was in high school. It would have made things more bearable."

"Well, we have each other now," I said. "And don't you ever forget it."

"So what about you, Grams? I heard that dad hired a caregiver to help you. How's that working out? Do you like her?

"Snoop-Face?" Noting Jeremy's quizzical expression, I quickly added, "Her name is Vera. She's a pain, but in all honesty, at least she gives me someone to vent my frustrations on – poor thing." I sat for a moment, realizing that I actually meant it. "You know, she's really not a bad person, either. Just a woman doing her job. It's this business of living in a place that operates like a military academy. I understand that we need structure and order for a number of reasons, but regimentation is stifling. It sucks all the excitement and fun out of life and, worst of all, it creates an atmosphere of resentment. At least, it does for me." I stopped for a moment, and then hurried on. "But I really don't want to talk about that with you. What I'd like to tell you is something that happened to me yesterday, or at least I think it happened. That's part of the problem."

I went on to share what I had experienced the previous night with the rainbow and my sudden sensation of taking flight. When I finished, Jeremy took my hand and held it tightly. "Was it exciting?" he asked, "this sensation of flying off into space??"

"Oh, yes . . . it was an amazing feeling! I actually felt alive for the first time in a very, very long time. But it could have been a hallucination, you know. Or a mini-stroke, or something." Before I could add anything else, Jeremy asked me a question I hadn't expected.

"Tell me, as a previous teacher what would you have said if one of your older students had come to you and told you a similar story, asking for your help? How would you have responded?

"Well," I said, considering his question carefully, "as safety is always a first consideration when working with people, I would have suggested that she see her doctor immediately, just to make sure she was physically OK."

"An excellent plan," he said. "And off the top of your head, what do you think – hypothetically, of course – of her experience? Did she imagine the whole thing, or was it real?"

"Oh, very real," I said quickly, forgetting that we were talking about a hypothetical person. Then, looking Jeremy directly in the eyes, I said, "You're having me on, aren't you?" I smiled at him.

"Grams, you're the sanest woman I know. If you tell me you had this experience, I believe you. Imagination is an amazing thing; it allows for freedom in ways that nothing else can. I know this as an artist. It can help us escape from stifling circumstances, breathing life back into our day-to-day lives. I've made quite a study of imagination, and it's pretty much an established fact that imagination can help people recover from depression, re-ignite passions, calm us, inspire us . . . the list goes on and on. As I recall, Einstein purportedly said that 'imagination is everything.' It is the preview for life's coming attractions. But whether he actually said it or not, I believe it's true."

"Yes," I agreed. "I loved the sensation of absolute freedom. But it was even more than that. It reminded me of a rather special poem you may have read." I went on to recite Magee's beautiful poem "High Flight," telling him about my early experience with the rainbow and repeating the story about the loss of my brother Jake.

Jeremy sat quietly, considering the words of the young poet. "I remember coming across the poem years ago, and I never forgot it. It gave me goose bumps at the time, and made me want to become a pilot. I love people who can paint pictures so powerfully with words." He sat lost in thought for the moment, and then said, "You know, you used the word *epiphany* when you told me about Magee's experience. What does the word really mean to you, at least when it isn't being used in reference to a Christian observance?"

I thought about that, then said, "Well, for me it means a sudden knowing, something that comes out of the blue and is felt at a visceral level . . . a kind of 'aha moment,' something that simply can't be denied."

I took out the iPhone Jeremy had given me and typed in *epiphany definition* and hit search. "According to Dictionary.com," I said, "it refers to 'an appearance or manifestation, especially of a deity.' It also refers to 'an intuitive perception of or an insight into the reality or essential meaning of something, usually initiated by some simple, homely, or commonplace occurrence or experience.'"

"Like the appearance of a rainbow, perhaps," Jeremy said, staring at me intently.

We spent the rest of the day together, visiting various landmarks including Seattle's central library made of soaring glass and steel. Somehow, it seemed the fitting end for our day. I arrived home exhausted and fell quickly to sleep. The day would remain one of transition and change for me.

Jeremy married several years later a wonderful man. They live in a beautiful old Victorian home in Port Townsend and have invited me to come live with them, but I have declined their kind offer. This is their time. Jeremy got his pilot's license recently, and he takes me up in their plane at least once a month. I have made my peace with Vera, although we still spar out of habit. And I have learned that my imagination can take me many places that only I can see. That's a good thing, actually, as flying has become a necessary part of my daily life.

This story is a work of fiction, but the details surrounding John Gillespie Magee's experiences in WWII are based in fact.

Author Intro

CRAIG ANDREWS

We all have our preferences. I am a writer. I write mostly about the magical moments in my life, usually concerning the natural world; but perhaps first, or should I say, "foremost," I am a poet.

Poetry walks the edge of creative feeling, creative thought, and creative expression. Its landscape is the remembered realness which travels through my own Mythological understanding of what Life and Self are truly about. My pen is my artist's brush. The words are all the colors of the rainbow, placed and positioned like a jazz rendition of reality.

My poems are descriptions of a world which I choose to see and pass on; but there is, I feel, a responsibility, for there is no defense for a well-crafted poem. It goes directly into the deeper layers of the psyche without so much as a pause. Yes, I am a college graduate, and I have had a life filled with more experiences than would stuff a suitcase, but in keeping with my desire to make my life a practice in ahimsa, I try to be kind.

Here then is an offering of my poetry. We will run the gambit from serious, through quizzical, to fun; and it is my sincere wish that you enjoy the ride.

All of Craig's books are available on Amazon.com in print and eBook format. He may be reached at tarasparkman@yahoo.com.

BEHOLDEN

One would dream of an Age of Kindness upon the Earth

When helpfulness and consideration fill the heart

As birdsong fills the drifting of the sky;

You and I have joined hands for the long walk

Pilgrims down a perilous road,

We have said that gladness is the soil from which all Life begins,

Let us be gardeners then;

There is a smile from which worlds are made

Dancing in the refrains of a flute which never repeats its song;

I Am Enchanted of you,

Shakti,

Wild creature of the Dawn.

BRAEWYN

For sixteen years I have combed your fleas,

For sixteen years I have been saying, "Drop it!

  No don't eat that!"

And for sixteen years I have been your coach,

  "Easy now laddie. Easy does it. Good! That will do."

As you herded geese, chased coyotes from the

  yard, and deer from the garden,

We are both getting older,

You sleep a lot now

And are covered with bumps,

Lord, I sure love you so.

CORE BELIEFS

Two days ago the dog pooped in the garden,

Yesterday I went out with the shovel to re-distribute the
offering

But it was not to be found,

I searched where I knew it was supposed to be,

I had carefully marked where it fell

Calculated the angle between two pots and a bean pole,

But no poop,

Today while planting the garlic I stepped squarely into the
center

  of the fragrant pile

Necessitating a deep cleaning of sandals and a resurgence of
  parasite phobia,

This is not an isolated occurrence!

This is yet another example of a dark humor in the very
  foundations of Life!

A basic absurdity which lurks in the Smile of God.

KENSHO

In the early morning rain

I watch deer walk by,

They are relaxed,

At home,

They nibble the grass and the flowers in our garden,

I gather up my rain boots

My big hat and coat

And prepare myself for our morning walk;

How did we ever get this way

Where we need to wear our comfort?

The deer are comfortable from the inside-out,

They grew-up in the trees,

They wear the sky,

We gave away our fat and our fur

Traded them for skins made from misery

And the enslavement of plants,

How did we ever think to come to this place?

Oh well, I shake my head,

One more latte will fix the show.

NANDI

Last night the coyotes came by the house,

They yipped and cavorted outside our bedroom window,

"Hey Farm dog! Come out and play! Hey Farm dog!"

"We know you are in there;

We know where you hide your bones,"

Our new dog sprang up in bed

Ears held high in Red Alert!

She growled,

She held the ground with her people,

She's a good dog.

NOVEMBER GRUMPS

I Am immersing my Self into a pond of glum,

Why Am I so ill treated as to be born again as a Human?

Haven't I moved beyond this!

What did I do wrong?

"But,"

You are so fond to point out,

"Only Human-Beings write poetry,"

"You don't know this!" I retort,

"Maybe the best poetry is done with scents,

 or sounds, or in ways that we don't understand,"

You shake your head and walk away,

I order a double espresso,

Sit by the window, and watch the rain.

ONE VIEW OF HEAVEN

We have a mouse in the kitchen,
We have, in-fact, a whole dynasty of mice
  who have passed through our kitchen;

Somewhere, deeply hidden, is a magic door
  And there is a dispenser on this door which reads,
  in mousenease, "Take a number - you will all be
  served,"
We, the God and Goddess of this realm, practice
  Ahimsa
But we have two grumpy cats and three mostly
  alert dogs who reside with us and do not speak
  Sanskrit,
The mice, when their number is called, pass through
  this hidden door and into a kingdom beyond their
  wildest dreams,
There are all matter of colorful and shiny things
  to play with and climb upon,
And there are foods of celestial wonder,
Cat food, desert crumbs, forgotten treats tucked
  away in corners, fruits of all kinds, and peanut
  butter and avocado!
There are places to scamper and places to hide
And the thrill of lurking Dragons,
And though their stay there may not last for
  many days, some I'm sure are legends (Old Tom
  Creeper - He lived there for a year and a-half),
They will eventually come face to face with the
  Cosmic Leveling Force,
For all which live must one day pass through
  That door
And even the Kitchen of the Gods
Will, in time, come to naught.

SOMEDAY

Someday,

Some very wealthy and

Very powerful person

Will take off his shoes and refuse to put them back on,

And any bank, grocery store, or restaurant which

 denies him service

Would lose his patronage and receive negative treatment

 from all of his friends, and all of his business partners,

 and all of their friends, etc.

And he will hire a team of very expensive lawyers

Who will contest the idea that the bottom of a persons'

 foot is any more unhealthy than the bottom of their

 shoes,

So soon other people will want to emulate this courageous

 but timely act

Will also take off their shoes,

And the freedom of this will spread across the world

That Human Beings will once again connect with

 their Mother Earth.

THE BRIGHT LANDS

I once watched a deer walk across a field and into

the brilliance of the afternoon Sun where my sight

was blinded and I could not see,

I changed the angle of my sight but the deer was gone

She had not come out of the Sun;

It is not a question of whether or not I believe in

The Bright Lands,

It is just what I know in my Heart

That the Beauty of this world reaches further

than I can see

And the tears I have shed in this life

Are a river which flows into that Sea,

And this I know,

That there is a place

Somewhere

Where the Sons and Daughters of the Light

Walk with empty hand.

THE DREAM

I had this dream:

You were gently pressed against me on my left side,

Cozy and warm,

And you were gently pressed against me on my right side,

Cozy and warm,

Your eyes were closed and your breathing was quiet and deep,

All your troubles had gone away

And I was held safe, and snuggled into the twin arms of you,

The Moon shown through our open window,

Somewhere, far off, the coyotes yipped in their own delight in the
   darkening night,

And I came to believe this, that the deep stillness of love is the
   root of all which is kind.

THE FLY

There is a fly walking across my forehead
As I sit immobile in my easy chair
Drifting in the heat of the Summer's afternoon
Barely alive
Exploring strange worlds,
Now he is walking around my elbow
He is unsure of whether to go up or down my arm,
My drifting is over
My eyes are still pasted shut
I don't want to move
But he has my full attention now
He is thinking of crawling up my nose,
God did not make flys
He would not do this to me,
Flys are the work of a fallen Angel,
In my older years of Dharma
In which I seek to show kindness to Life
I no longer own a fly swatter
But I Am thinking of one,
Oh well,
Perhaps he was only sent to remind me to prepare the
dinner
Of which he will, no doubt, receive a small portion in return.

THE OLD MAN AND THE MOUNTAIN
A Parable

An old man walks up the path to the mountain
from the valley below,
As he walks, his mind is at peace
Reflecting only the wind, the sun, and the cries of
the high circling birds;

A young man trudges up the same mountain path,
His legs ache from the climb
And his mind is in turmoil
Spinning with questions and opinions,
Whirling with the speed of the dust devils in the fields
below;

As he continues up the mountain
The young man will come upon the old man
Resting by the side of the trail
And he will sense a special quality about him
As one would sense a Sage;

He will ask the old man many questions
Feeling, perhaps, that Heaven has guided him to this
meeting;
The old man will not be able to help him though
For the old man thinks nothing,
And there is no room for "nothing" in the young man's mind.

THIS THING WHICH HAPPENS

It's this thing which happens to Human Beings,

The Autumn Sun which lays upon the skin

Like warm honey from the lips of God

And the quickening of the day in every shade of green,

  purple, and golds,

Insects traversing the air in counter point

To the calls of a thousand birds,

  The distant song of a coyote wandering home,

And then as you stand transfixed mouth agape

Tears running down your cheeks for the beauty of it all

The one you love comes up behind you and places their

  hand upon your shoulder,

And you know that there is nothing left to do

But melt into Life.

WISTFULLY

Once upon a time
I reached out and shyly touched the fingers of a beautiful maid,
And she responded by gently taking my hand in her own,
If the world had stopped then, we would be Angels now,
And together in peace.

Author Intro

ELIZABETH K. PRATT

After moving to the Olympic Peninsula in 2005, I found new passions to pursue and a new career path to follow. There are few outdoor opportunities that I've left untried: from biking the Olympic Discovery Trail to kayaking on Lake Crescent, from fishing off the rocks in Neah Bay to digging clams at Sequim Bay, from hiking to Sol Duc Falls, to taking the drive to the top of Blue Mountain. But, when the winter storms blow in, you can find me cozy at home with my three rescue cats, often with a pen in hand, or practicing on my violin for concerts with the Sequim Community Orchestra.

I work with local senior citizens and their families to find safe, healthy living options, create special events for residents, and speak at local events about the benefits of assisted living communities. One of my pieces in this anthology, "Rolling Thunder," is the story of one such event, a bucket list activity crossed off the list of a 104-year-old woman. While I usually write fiction grown from a single nugget of truth, the stories I write about resident experiences are memories I love to share.

Beth can be reached at beth132@gmail.com

EAT OR BE EATEN

She dropped her bike in the breezeway, the crash of metal on concrete echoed into the house. Not just Grandma's house anymore. Now it was her home, too.

"Grandma? Are you here?" Pearl called.

"Come in the kitchen, Pearl. I could use a hand," Grandma Kae replied.

The fifteen-year-old noted the steamed windows and humid heat rolling through the French doors. Then she saw that the boxes of tomatoes from the breezeway worktable were gone. Canning day was here.

"Grandma! Why didn't you tell me this morning? I would have come straight home instead of going to the library," Pearl said, racing to drop her coat and backpack in her bedroom.

"You're here now, so grab an apron. I've blanched all the red ones, so get ready to peel." Grandma Kae, tidy in her bright, flowered smock stepped to the side, making a workspace for Pearl.

They stood over the sink, drain plugged to contain the skins and keep them out of the sensitive septic system. Each had a giant bowl of tomatoes in ice water. Working in silence, they squeezed the fruit gently to release the skin and dropped the naked tomatoes into a third bowl, shining clean steel.

Pearl relaxed into the rhythm of work. She loved to help with the summer canning. Her grandmother put up dozens upon dozens of jars filled with jewel-colored delights: peaches golden like citrine, mint pears green as jade, berries and cherries like rubies and garnets. Then the preserves, chutneys, jams and soups, most of which were put up in the fall. Pearl's favorite chutney was the Green Tomato Soy, a

"Victory Gardens" recipe from WWII, which strangely contained no soy products at all.

"Do you have enough green ones left for Soy?" she asked as she rinsed the last of the papery-thin skin from her fingers.

Kae smiled indulgently, "Of course. In the northwest, we always have plenty of green tomatoes. Why fried green tomatoes have only just caught on here, well, it's beyond me."

"Are we going to make it today?" They had used the last jar in June, and fried eggs were not the same without it.

"Not today. I think this will do for one day's work," Kae spread her arms as if to hold the dozens of jars and bushels of tomatoes.

"Tomorrow?" Pearl persisted. Kae pulled the steaming hot Ball jars from the warm oven and began filling them with the pulpy fruit.

"Oh, alright. We'll do the Soy tomorrow. The Granny Smith's aren't quite ready for pie filling and the pears have some time to go yet." Kae chuckled lightly at the girl's enthusiasm. "It amazes me, your excitement over canning. Your mother couldn't be bothered to pick, let alone can, a single piece of fruit. But she could eat!" Kae's smile grew sad when she spoke of her only daughter, gone for nearly a year.

"I dunno why, but I love to help. You know, I won't eat those things they serve at school. They call 'em peaches, but yuck! When we get done, we have so much. And I like to eat, too." Pearl grinned as she snatched a raw tomato from the window sill and bit into it like it was an apple. "Where's the salt shaker?" she mumbled around her mouthful.

"Oh, honestly, Pearl, it is all over your face." Kae swiped playfully at her with the kitchen towel. "Salt is over by the door. I did some slug extermination today." She shook the cardboard canister of salt at Pearl like a maraca, then began adding a little to each jar.

"Grandma! You salted the slugs?" Pearl was aghast. "That is so brutal!"

"Oh, Pearl, they are barely more than plants. Anyway, how do you think I keep these gardens going? Magic? Poison and salt are two of a gardener's best friends."

Pearl considered this while she finished her tomato. "Maurice and Matilda across the street, they put out pie plates full of beer for the slugs. Does that just put them to sleep?"

"No, it drowns them. They crawl in and can't get back out."

"Oh. I guess that isn't any better, is it?"

"It's eat or be eaten, Pearl-girl.

"What does Pastor Mark do?"

"God knows, Pearl. He isn't exactly giving gardening lessons during the Sunday sermon. But, according to Velma Shaw, he is always asking the ladies in the auxiliary for advice. The way she tells it, it isn't just gardening tips he's after."

Pearl was always fascinated by the gossip Velma spread so freely, like she knew more than everyone else in this town. How could anyone know more than everything about everyone? Behind her back, the other ladies at the Methodist Church said you could lock yourself away in the deepest cellar and clear your throat quietly and within twelve hours, Velma Shaw would be on your step with a bouquet from Muriel's Flower Shop and a date for the fundraiser that would pay your hospital bills.

"You know Velma makes half of that up, don't you, Pearl?" Kae asked the girl, her brow creased in the middle, her words coming slowly.

Laughing, Pearl said, "Of course! Some of the stories she comes up with clash with ones she told before. You would think that she could keep track of her own tales. But what about Arlene? She seems to know a lot about everyone, though she isn't so quick to tell anyone who will listen, is she?" Pearl asked.

"Here, take these rings. Don't tighten them too much." Kae took a moment before she answered the question. "Arlene isn't malicious. She isn't trying to be anything, or do anything, with what she knows. She just likes to know, and will share her knowledge with anyone who needs it and comes to her for help. I think Velma is just trying to make herself into some kind of Queen Bee, but no one has the heart to tell her she isn't. That's why it's different."

Different, like green tomatoes and red tomatoes. Like her life before and after the accident. Her mother was gone, but Grandma Kae was here. Different lives, different kinds of love, but room for both in her heart.

ROLLING THUNDER

Bright yellow roses bloom along the entry to the retirement community. The open park and pond, surrounded by walking paths and shade trees, is a space for a quiet stroll or to sit and reflect. Except for the day the thunder came to visit. It rolled down the driveway and around the fountain as seventeen Harley Davidson's and their riders arrived. Elgin had been brought to the front to watch the arrival.

They came for her.

As they rolled passed, one at a time, her eyes dewed and her smile widened by the second.

Each rider waved to her as they passed, revving their engines for her. They parked in a tight formation as her blue chariot rolled to a stop in front of her. Before they lowered their kickstands, Diana reached up one hand from Elgin's wheelchair and gave the cue. They opened their throttles. The roar and rumble pouring form those big pipes echoed through the parking lot and bounced off the buildings.

Tears of joy rolled down Elgin's ancient cheeks. This day was all for her.

In May, the opportunity to fly in a hot air balloon had awakened Elgin's adventurous spirit. She had been proud to learn that she was the oldest person, at 104 ½, to fly in a hot air balloon. The day after the flight, she told one of her caregivers, "You know, I've always wanted to ride in a motorcycle gang. I want to hear the thunder. Feel it." She told the right person. Diana belongs to a Harley club.

The Hooligans, with a few friends from the Amigos and the Riggin' Rats, rallied together to grant this wish of an elder they did not know. They came to meet her, just a few of them, and to invite her to ride with them. The date was set and the news crews decided to come and report the story.

For three weeks, preparations were underway. Elgin received gifts from the club: a new Harley shirt, sparkling with sequins; an official black and red Hooligans t-shirt; a Harley patch for her wheelchair. Then, a visit to the local 'cycle shop for a helmet and leathers to keep her safe.

The news crews came early to interview Elgin, to learn about her past before telling the story of her present. She told them that she had not been on a motorcycle in 93 years, since her father had given up his Indian with a sidecar in favor of a Model T, around 1925.

The day came and the thunder, the sound Elgin had longed for, rolled for her. With gentle formality, Diana wheeled her to meet her new family. They had another gift to give before her ride, a new patch for her wheelchair. This one said, "Harley Mama."

It took two aids to dress Elgin in her leathers and helmet. Once attired, cameras flashing and video rolling, five members of the club, themselves geared in black leather accented in red, lifted her to the seat behind her driver, Wayne. Her smile became a smirk as they lowered her visor and fired up the engine.

Elgin's blue Harley led, sixteen bikes falling in line behind her as the pack departed. The echo of their engines was a "See you soon!" to the audience left behind.

Chase cars followed the pack. The clubs were well practiced in group riding, blocking intersections to keep everyone together through red lights and stop signs.

Their path was pre-determined, with Ediz Hook their destination. They would stop at the boat launch and give the news crews time to get more footage, talk with Elgin, and duct tape a GoPro camera to the back of Wayne's jacket to get close-up shots of Elgin's face.

Someone said, "She wants to go her age!" Several of the men put their heads together. Diana suggested, "You better ask her daughter!"

Elgin's daughter was in one of the chase cars. "She can do whatever she wants. It's up to her!"

Permission granted.

Direction and discussion were invisible to those who watched. The wives and girlfriends hopped off the backs of the bikes. Less weight, more speed. Chase cars and a few riders raced back down the road. Road blocks deployed.

With a rumble, the Harleys fired their engines and raced. The growl of redline-level RPMs boomed out across the Strait. Elgin's blue ride, the only bike with two riders, blended into the pack.

Another round of interviews and camera angles. A deep voice said, "I topped out at 95." A woman's voice answered, "Don't tell her. Let her think she went 104."

Elgin's motorcycle gang took a longer route home, parading their newly adopted matriarch through all of Port Angeles. Club members were placed strategically through town to capture the event in picture and video. Thanks to social media, the people of Port Angeles were out, too, watching for the riders, supporting the efforts of local people doing something special for a senior citizen who asked.

While the story of Elgin's ride is one of joy, giving and kindness, it is more than that. The Hooligans lost one of their own to a terrible accident. A young woman, barely out of high school, had died only one week before this ride. A beloved daughter, niece, sister, aunt – she had gone for a ride with her new motorcycle endorsement, her driving her mother's bike and her father behind on his. She would never return. The Hooligans had broken hearts. They were burdened with the sorrow of untimely loss. But they never even considered cancelling on Elgin. They chose to give, to offer her joy. They chose to honor their lost daughter by giving this gift to their new Hooligan Mama.

When they brought Elgin home, they gave her another resounding blast of Harley thunder. Above the din, she shouted "NO!" as the men leaned in to lift her from that beautiful, blue bike.

Elgin was still glowing the next day, her patches arranged on the back of her wheelchair, wearing her Hooligan's t-shirt. Someone asked her what she would do next. "I heard there is a hang glider that lands on wheels, like a wheelchair."

Elgin isn't done with the thunder. Riding in it wasn't enough. Time to fly.

FALLEN

Meal time rhythms were already becoming familiar. First, Kurt would arrive and take the wingback chair by the fireplace. Then, Lucille and Theo would come and park their canes against the wall before taking seats around the coffee table. Sylvia, Helen, and Hardin would often sit on the seats of their walkers to await the opening of the dining room doors.

"Once you get to know them a little, you'll be able to tell when someone is missing. Dinner is when we often find them." My trainer gave me a knowing, raised-eyebrow look and lowered her voice. "You know, find them in trouble."

I nodded, trying for indifference while I processed her words. Find them in trouble. With an average age hovering in the mid-80s and our oldest resident north of 100, trouble meant one of only a few things, none of them good.

During my third and final interview, I had almost decided to walk away from the job. Tales of bodily fluids and emergency first aid were nearly too much. Death and serious medical events had not seemed nearly as scary as vomit.

But, I reasoned, how often would any of that happen, really? At the end of Week One, I had experienced a work environment that felt like a luxury hotel where all the guests were elderly. Big deal. I came from a large family, with more than 20 great aunts and uncles. I could handle an occasional special event.

Sudden chaos in the dining room entry interrupted my reflection. A small woman lay on the floor, her walker on its side, and her husband was bent over, dangerously off balance, to reach a hand to her.

"Call 911!" my trainer directed. "And pull Helen Summer's emergency card."

I called, I pulled the card, and I watched my trainer. My instructions for my first emergency were to simply observe and follow any directions given, but to stay out of the way. So I did.

The other residents continued to pour into the dining room, the flow of people breaking like water around a stone, giving Helen the little space where she lay.

Helen and George Summers were both in their mid-90s, and Helen was a tiny, frail woman. Medical events like cancer and lung disease had taken their toll. She might have weighed 100 pounds, but I doubted it. Her bony body was all sharp angles beneath her kitten-applique sweatshirt.

"Get me up!" Helen insisted to my trainer. "I'm not hurt. Just get me up!"

My trainer answered with an almost-whine, her hands fluttering around like they wanted to do something but had no idea as to what that might be. "Helen, I can't lift you. We aren't allowed. Can you get up on your own?" Her eyes kept darting to the entry doors, panic was spreading over her features. I could almost see the word bubble over her head, "Where are the EMTs?!?"

"Just get me on my feet, I'm not hurt," Helen insisted. George chimed in, "Get her up." His soft, patient voice was almost forceful.

"You know the rules, I can't do that." My trainer was like a teenager telling an adult no for the first time.

Residents weren't the only people at dinner. Lance King's son, Chris, was visiting from Colorado with his family and they were already at the salad bar.

Chris King was giant of a man, at least 6'4" with a big, round belly and hands that could palm a soccer ball. He butted in.

"Why don't you get her up?" he demanded with police-like authority, looming over my kneeling trainer. "She said she isn't hurt."

"We aren't allowed to lift them, Chris. The EMTs are coming." Her answer was more apology than explanation. She stood. "She'll be OK. They'll be here in just a minute to help her."

"You should help her!" Chris had a big voice to match his oversized presence. The dining room buzz went nearly silent, only those too deaf to hear him still clinking silverware against plates. "Isn't that what everyone here pays for? Help!?!"

My trainer stared down at her feet, shuffling back a little. "We aren't medical staff," she mumbled, taking another step backward.

Chris had no more words. In one swift motion, he bent down, slid his hands under Helen's armpits from behind, held her back to his front and lifted.

But he didn't set her on her feet. He held her against his body as he stood, her back bowing against his round belly, her tiny feet in their bright white Keds dangling near his knees.

Staring and silent, my trainer had no more words, either.

Chris turned left and right, looking for something. With a flash of understanding, I called to my trainer, "Get a chair!" She snapped into some kind of focus and scrambled around the fallen walker to drag a chair over for the dangling woman.

The big man set Helen down and, without another word, chest puffed out, strode back to the salad bar.

My trainer righted Helen's walker as the red lights of approaching aid cars strobed through the foyer.

I prompted her, "Maybe a chair for George, too?" Moving like a sleepwalker, she slid another chair over. George sat and reached to hold Helen's hand.

"Here is her information," I handed one of the EMTs the little card. "We had a guest step in and help her up, into the chair."

My trainer stayed with Helen, George and the EMTs while they checked the frail, old woman for injuries. I wondered if her back would ache from being bent over Chris's belly.

The whole fiasco resulted in Helen and George continuing into dinner. Only fifteen minutes had passed, and the room had returned to normal.

"Well, I guess we got you trained in handling emergencies. Falls are the most common." My trainer attempted to reassert her authority. "You'll be able to handle dinner on your own next week."

"Yeah, good to learn by doing," I answered, almost succeeding in hiding my new-found lack of respect. There were a lot of lessons to learn from that fifteen minutes, none of them taught on purpose.

Helen and George lived out their lives, and probably never thought again about the time Helen tripped going in for dinner and Chris King picked her up. But I do. Every time I attend to a resident who has fallen, I see those tiny, white Keds dangling midair.

Author Intro

KIRSTI LEE

I was born and raised in West Seattle in a large family of outdoors people. My father was a lumberman and fisherman who retired from the Carlsborg Mill in the early 1960s. My mother was an avid gardener and artist.

My family spent many days on the Olympic Peninsula, in the Strait, and on the San Juan Islands as children. The Salish Sea was our playground.

When I retired from property management after many years away, I returned home to Washington from Chicagoland in 2017. Sequim felt like home the moment I arrived. The beauty of the Olympic Peninsula has not lost its shine from my childhood memories. I have had, since childhood, a deep and loving respect for nature and her creatures. My connection to these creatures is an integral part of me.

I am grateful for the opportunity to share with others my love of and the joy I receive each day living on the Olympic Peninsula, via the Olympic Peninsula Authors.

Kirsti can be reached at kirsti54@yahoo.com

QUIETLY SPOKEN, QUIETLY SUNG

The smells of the earth
And the moss that it grew
Warmed by the light of each morn
Born anew.

A mixture of sweetness
And shadowy mold
Greens as of jewels
And the softest of golds.

We whispered, we sang
We danced in the wind
With sun-dappled branches
And leaves that were brimmed.

With the glow of the sunlight
Awakening dawn
The Sentinels
Waiting in towering brawn.

Softly, so softly
The voices began
Will you walk here among us,
Child of Man?

We thrived through the ages
Our memories long
The mountains and rivers
Joined in our song.

A sad, lonely lesson
That has not been learned
About damage and loss
And a forest that burned.

We were counted in board foot
Not in lives lost
We stand here, we wait
We reckon the cost.

She listened, she walked
Her ragged breath drawn
She was told, they're just trees
Life just goes on.

She heard them
The Sentinels, deep in her soul
Her heart plunged in shadow
Truly broken, unwhole.

Quietly spoken, quietly sung
She heard them all singing
Its resonance hung

From the air, from the air
All around her it swept
As she silently listened
And, silently, wept.

THE DANCE

The dance in the sky at first light
fills the air with their passion for flight.

The sun shines on their wings and sets them aglow.
They spin and they dive and they feast as they go.

The song in the sky at first light
fills the air with their voice of delight.

They fly and they sing, full of joy the songs ring.
Every note filled with life as they herald in spring
with their dance of their flight at the first of the light.

Author Intro

JACK BARNES

I suppose like most people who write fiction, I began reading at an early age and soon began trying to write stories of my own. The first thing actually published was a semi-suspense story in a high school literary magazine in the middle of the last century. I worked my way through college as a lab technician in the early days of transistors, and logically enough wound up with a technical degree, math in my case. That job and a subsequent one as an aerospace tech writer kept me writing non-fiction for more than a decade. Eventually I went back to grad school and earned a couple of degrees in anthropology, which provided the background for the story included here.

I also went back to fiction writing, but the market for short fiction had changed drastically and was rapidly vanishing. However, in the late 1970s I finally published a suspense story in a paying market. A couple of years later I published another in a small magazine, long defunct now.

I've now been retired for more than a few years and I continue to write fiction largely for fun.

Jack Barnes can be reached at jabarnes9@gmail.com

WHO GOES THERE?

Alex Lawson was a frustrated man. He looked around the gloomy forest and frowned at the autumn drizzle. Olympic National Park was a spectacular chunk of real estate in good, or even tolerable, weather. It was also partly temperate rain forest, with the emphasis on "rain." Still, he had a paying job in his chosen profession, not easy for someone with a mere bachelor's degree in anthropology. He was conscientious enough to do it right, even though he considered it a fool's errand. Alex crested a small ridge and looked down into a typical valley, mostly forested but with brush and grass in a few open spots. He raised his binoculars and swept the area . . . and froze.

"What the hell!" he muttered. A vaguely manlike shape was visible at the edge of the trees. The creature, assuming it was real and not his imagination, must have had incredible hearing. It instantly turned to face him, then melted into the forest.

Alex shook his head, then moved quickly downslope. At the spot where he'd seen . . . something, he studied the ground carefully. He didn't consider himself a great tracker, but he was experienced enough to recognize the signs of someone, or something, having disturbed the leaf litter. After a moment he thought he could tell where "it" had entered the forest. There was nothing like a footprint, but the disturbed litter was clear for a few yards, then all signs vanished. Alex began to walk outward from the last marks in an increasing spiral. After six circles and an estimated fifty yards out, he admitted he was stymied. Either whatever he had seen was superior in terms of woodcraft – not unlikely – or he'd been hallucinating. He retraced his steps looking up into the trees. It was already too dark to see above the lowest branches. Clearly it was time to give it up for the day.

Back in camp he wondered what to say in the daily report due in just over an hour. He was not sure he hadn't imagined the whole thing, and he didn't want to get Kirby all excited over nothing. On the other hand, it was Kirby's project and Kirby's money. He had a right to know what was happening . . . if anything really had happened.

When Alex entered Eastern Washington University, just west of Spokane, he had no real idea of a major. Like his parents and most of his friends, he simply assumed going to college was a good idea.

His first quarter was typical of most "undecided" students and included a range of classes, one of which was anthropology. Alex was hooked before the term was even half over, and promptly declared his major. He was assigned to an advisor, a woman fairly well known in the field. She warned him he was training to be unemployed unless he got at least an M.A., and a doctorate would probably be required. Alex was undeterred, even after the Twin Towers came down and he spent four years in the military. Home again, he continued his studies.

As predicted almost eight years earlier, upon graduation Alex had zero luck finding any job related to anthropology, or any job at all other than flipping burgers or mowing lawns. Then the miracle: an ad appeared in the *Port Townsend Leader*, which his advisor subscribed to because it was her home town paper. She promptly passed it along to him:

Field researcher wanted for long term project. The successful applicant will have a degree in anthropology or a related field, be comfortable living and working in the outdoors, and have good communication skills. Field experience a plus, but not required. Email: proj12c1@gmail.com.

The resume Alex sent was as polished as he could make it while fitting on one page. He had been warned that a beginner did not have enough useful experience to write more than that without resorting to obvious padding. He stressed his service in Afghanistan and Iraq between 2002 and 2006 before he returned to school to complete his degree. While he had not done any formal fieldwork in anthropology, he had served in two Muslim countries and interacted with the local people in mainly peaceful and cooperative situations. His formal training had provided a general orientation in all aspects of anthropology. Finally, he emphasized that he had spent much time hiking, climbing, and backpacking from his early teens.

The morning after he emailed the resume there was a response from one Kirby Tammen in Port Townsend, forty miles west of Seattle on the Olympic Peninsula. He invited Alex to come for an interview as soon as he could get away. Alex could get away almost immediately, and the following day found him talking to Tammen in a restored Victorian mansion in Port Townsend. The man appeared to be in his fifties, and seemed ordinary enough except that he walked with a cane and a noticeable limp.

Once they introduced themselves and were provided with coffee, Tammen's first question was, "Tell me what you think you know about Sasquatch, Mr. Lawson."

Whatever Alex expected, that was nowhere near a beginning he was prepared for. "I think it's a myth," he said slowly. "No one has ever provided a photograph that didn't look fake, much less the obviously faked film back in the sixties."

Tammen nodded.

"I don't think we've identified every animal on the planet," Alex continued. "But a large mammal, and a primate at that, seems unlikely to have remained hidden all this time."

"True enough. But previously unknown large primates have come to light in remote areas in both South America and the South Pacific in recent decades. And they're our own species."

Alex wasn't sure where this was all going. "Yes, but they weren't living in close proximity to a large number of other humans. And in both the Philippines and the Amazon they weren't hidden from the people who did live nearby. They were just hidden from us, not from everyone."

Tammen nodded. "Clearly you've thought about it at least. Anything else?"

"The major issue to me is diet. What do these seven foot tall, four hundred pound primates eat? If they're carnivores, they'd be taking livestock sooner or later, and of all the things a rancher won't tolerate, someone or something eating his stock tops the list. And if they're vegetarians, what do they eat in the winter? The high country in this part of the world is pretty barren once the snow flies. I'm sorry, Mr. Tammen, but I just can't get my head around the notion of monster apes or ape-men, hiding in the Olympics or the Cascades."

"You may well be right. Let me tell you about the project I'm proposing and then we'll see if we can agree on investigating the possibilities."

Alex relaxed back in his chair. Tammen talked almost non-stop for the next twenty minutes. He had clearly thought out what he wanted to do and how to go about it and admitted he'd like to do the field work himself. He tapped the bad leg with a rueful smile. The field researcher would have a largely free hand as to how he did the work. He would be expected to visit places where sightings had been reported over the past twenty years or so, and talk to as many of the people who'd made the reports as could be located. If and when new sightings were reported he would check them out thoroughly. In addition, he'd survey likely spots for the hypothesized Sasquatches to live. Besides looking for the creatures themselves, he'd also keep an eye peeled for any other evidence, from tracks to scat to possible campsites.

At the end of it, Tammen grinned. "As you can tell, I'm semi-convinced there is something out there, despite your logical arguments to the contrary. Shall we talk any further, or do you want to forget it?"

Alex shrugged. "I've come a long ways and taken up your time. You might as well lay out the whole thing."

"Okay. I'll provide housing and equipment, including a four-wheel drive vehicle, and routine expenses. I'll also pay one thousand dollars a month, along with Social Security and health insurance. I can arrange with the Park Service for permission to travel and camp most anywhere in the back country. I'd like to cover the northern half of Olympic National Park from Forks around to Brinnon, at least initially." He paused for comments.

"Why the Olympics?" Alex asked. "The Cascades are a much larger area and possible sightings are probably more frequent over there."

"True. But the smaller area is easier to deal with, and since it's almost all National Park, there's less development and more solitude to hide in." Again he paused.

"It's going to cost hell's own amount of money," Alex said, lacking anything else to say.

Tammen grinned. "Actually, I have hell's own amount of money. I developed a gizmo that makes satellite phones truly secure. I leased the rights to some people with more money than God, and got a chunk of it." When Alex made no comment, he went on. "Well, what do you think? Even if you're a total skeptic it might be interesting for a year or so. In fact, a total skeptic would be better, because you'd have no incentive to fake it."

Alex thought for only a few seconds. "Okay, Mr. Tammen. I'm in."

Tammen laughed aloud and offered his hand. "Great. Welcome aboard, Alex. Call me Kirby. When can you start?"

Over the next fourteen months Alex saw more of the northern half of Olympic National Park than even the Park Rangers. He also met a number of people who had reported seeing Sasquatch, or finding tracks, or hearing strange and scary noises in the night. Many of them struck him as operating short of a full deck, but a few were earnest and puzzled rather than defensive or aggressive.

Unfortunately, none of his efforts – time on the ground, interviews, rereading official and news reports – brought him any closer to verifying the existence of anything not already known. He mostly enjoyed the work in the field, despite the rain and drizzle. The library and Internet and newspaper morgue parts of the process were good training for a budding scholar, as were the interviews.

Alex and Kirby Tammen became friends well beyond any employer-employee connection. They were both lonely; Kirby was recently widowed and Alex knew no one else on the Peninsula. It was only that friendship that kept Alex on the job after a year. He felt he was wasting his time and Kirby's money. He had decided to tell Kirby he'd hang it up after the weather got truly unpleasant, but today left him uncertain.

A glance at his watch showed he had spent his hour of grace woolgathering and vacillating. He got out the secure phone Kirby had given him, insisting Alex call every day while he was in the field. Granted that Alex was experienced, things could go wrong and if Kirby didn't hear from him, the assumption would be that something had.

Alex remained unsure what to say as the phone rang. As usual, Kirby answered after a single ring. "Hello, Alex. How are things? Other than wet, that is."

"Pretty much the same, including wet." Alex decided it wouldn't hurt Kirby to wait a day or two before getting him all excited or reporting another failure.

"It's got to be uncomfortable. Why don't you come back to civilization until the weather gets better?"

Alex chuckled. "That's likely to happen sometime next May. This is Wednesday, so I'll give it tomorrow and be back Friday afternoon."

"Okay, if you say so. Come by my place about five and I'll supply drinks and dinner."

Alex had trouble getting to sleep that night. If he had seen a Sasquatch and — an even bigger if — he was able to verify it, he'd make a major professional contribution first thing out of the box. If he couldn't verify it he became just another nut. During the night the wind came up and whipped his tent fabric loudly enough to wake him. He peered outside to find the rain had ended and the sky was starry. Alex went back to sleep.

Breakfast was coffee and an energy bar. He was anxious to get back to the place he'd seen . . . whatever he'd seen. Kirby had supplied a high tech video camera along with everything else. Alex quit carrying it after finding nothing to shoot in the first month, but this time he put it into his daypack.

The day was sunny and quite warm for October, but the windstorm had done more damage than Alex expected. Lots of limbs and smaller branches littered the ground. When he crested what he thought of as "Bigfoot Ridge," he stopped and raised the binoculars. He was disappointed but not surprised to see nothing in the clearing. He moved carefully down the slope and into the trees where the "whatever" had disappeared. He walked slowly down the valley in the direction his quarry had apparently headed. After perhaps two hundred yards he came to another clear spot. Fifty feet away something brown and furry was lying under a large limb blown from a nearby red cedar.

Alex stared for at least thirty seconds before moving forward. He squatted on his heels beside the unmoving form, shoved aside a branch, and found himself face to face with Sasquatch. "Oh . . . My . . . God," he breathed.

He couldn't tell if the creature was alive or dead. There was no sign of chest movement, the eyes were half-closed and appeared blank. After another long pause he touched the fur on the nearest shoulder. All the reports said the beasts were covered with long hair, often described as reddish brown. This one was simply medium brown, and the fur was short. It felt more like plush than an animal's coat. The skin under the fur didn't have the chill of death.

Alex pulled out the video camera and shot a twenty second close-up of the face and head. Then he moved some way back and stuck the camera's monopod in the ground. Making sure the zoom was set to take in the entire body, he turned it on and phoned Kirby. "I've got the video camera running and it should be transmitting to your server. Please check and be sure." He closed the phone and stepped in front of the camera. He gave Kirby a few seconds to reach the monitor, then asked, "Okay?"

"Sound and picture," Kirby said over the video link. "My God!" he gasped when Alex stepped aside.

"Indeed. Stay tuned."

Alex lifted the limb far enough to see most of what was under it.

"Sank you." The voice was sibilant but the words were clear.

Alex didn't quite drop the limb. He'd been watching the face and the lips had not moved. With what he considered great aplomb, he shifted the limb to get most of the weight off the body. "Who are you?" he asked.

"I am the . . . entity directing this vehicle." The voice improved with every word, as though the "entity" had not used it in a long time. "You can call me Alien. You are?"

"Pleased to meet you Alien. I'm Alex." Only later when he watched the recording did he realize how fatuous that sounded. "You mean to tell me this . . . this animal is a vehicle? Something like a robot?"

"Exactly. The . . . tree fell last night and damaged it severely." This time, listening closely, Alex could tell the voice was coming from the middle of the Sasquatch's chest. "It is quite strong normally, but one arm and leg are damaged so badly it can get no . . . power?"

"Leverage?" Alex suggested.

"Exactly. No leverage. I am grateful to you for your help. Within a short time the vehicle will be able to move and I shall depart."

"Uh, not quite. I want to know who you are, where you're from, why you're here, and a lot more."

After a silence long enough to make Alex wonder if the alien was going to clam up, the voice continued. "I suppose that is fair, since you may have saved my life." Again, a long pause. "I am a . . . a being from a long way off. The star which my home circles is not visible from here without a large instrument. I am here because my . . . species has a very different sort of life path from yours. For the first half of our lives we are exceedingly social. We perform useful and creative tasks, raise the next generation, and in many ways are similar to humans. After that, though, we become increasingly solitary and avoid our own kind. Some turn to what you would call philosophy and sequester themselves in remote places on our home planet or nearby. Others enjoy visiting and studying other life forms. We seldom interact with those other life forms except by accident as in this situation."

"How did you get here? And how long have you been coming? The stories about your 'vehicles' go back many generations."

"We travel by ship, and it takes a long time. But we live a long time. We have a base on the far side of your moon."

"But the other side of the moon has been overflown and photographed for decades."

"True, but we are well hidden. And there has been little interest in recent years. As for how long, I have been here more than a century of your time. I shall return home soon to spend my last years with my descendants. This is the third stage of our lives. My predecessors have visited here for about three thousand of your years."

The phone Alex had stuck in his pocket was vibrating fit to shake him off his feet. "Yes, Kirby," he said impatiently.

"I'm on my way there. Don't let him take off before I arrive."

Alex's phone had GPS capabilities, so Kirby knew within a few yards where he and the alien were. "It's pretty far into the backcountry," he said tactfully. He didn't want to remind Kirby of his bad leg.

"I know where it is. There's a service road less than two miles away. With any luck I should be there inside an hour. Just make sure the alien doesn't take off. If necessary drop the limb back on him."

"I'm not sure . . ." Alex began. He was going to suggest that would not be the best way to conduct the first meeting between extraterrestrials and humans, but thought better of it. " . . . that will be necessary," he finished lamely.

"How do you come to speak English so well?" he asked Alien.

"The vehicle has a variety of sensors and machines capable of recording virtually everything it experiences. It took a long time in early years to learn languages, but now that you use extensive electronic communications it is very easy. Likewise, your television and Internet allow us to view a wide variety of real and imaginary situations. We have gained significant insight into your ways of life."

Alex realized he was dealing with an alien anthropologist, albeit an amateur one. Somehow it made him more comfortable with the situation. "If you have this instinct, or need, or whatever it is to be solitary, how can you be at ease in this case?"

"The need to withdraw declines as this life-phase passes. Since I am near the end of it the problem is lessened."

"Then why not make yourself known? Can't you imagine how humans would welcome proof that we aren't alone in the universe?"

Again there was a lengthy pause. The voice, which Alex was sure had to be artificial, actually sounded pedantic when Alien spoke. "More than a century ago was The War of the Worlds. Aliens were evil. In The Day the Earth Stood Still, the alien was benign, but humans felt threatened anyway. More recently, Star Trek, both movies and TV painted aliens as potentially threatening. And the aliens in Independence Day were 'a plague.' We have no wish to make any or all humans frightened or hostile. It is better to remain hidden."

Alex started to argue that those examples were all fiction, but in fact it was true that most humans were xenophobic . . . the only real variable was how the 'other' was defined. Alex asked more questions and got only general answers. Clearly Alien was getting tired of cooperating and more than ready to put an end to it. Then Alex's phone vibrated again. "Now what, Kirby?"

"Sorry, Alex. I'm in trouble. I was making good progress until I stepped into a hole of some sort and the bad leg just gave up on me."

"Where are you?"

"About a half mile south and a tad east of you. Bring your phone so I can guide you when you get close."

"Okay, I'm on my way. Hang in there, Kirby."

"Don't worry, I plan to. Don't let your new friend get away."

Alex turned to Alien. "You heard?"

"Yes. I can try to stay, but although talking to one human is possible, the idea of two or more is discomfiting."

Alex didn't know what to say to that, so he nodded and headed for where he thought Kirby was waiting. It took less than half an hour. He found Kirby semi-sitting up, one leg twisted partway under him. His cane was several feet away and he looked to be in no little pain.

"Just get my stick and help me up, please."

Alex did as directed. Once the older man was upright, he was able to put a little weight on the bad leg, but it was clear any traveling was going to be slow indeed. Kirby had put his phone away as Alex helped him up. Now he pulled it out again and connected to the video from the camera.

They watched as Alien stood up slowly and limped a few steps. The limp vanished. Alien then swung an arm several times, until it too seemed to function properly.

After a look around, Alien walked to the camera until head and chest filled the frame. "I am happy to have met you Alex. And I will always be grateful for your assistance. Alas, I cannot stay to meet your colleague. But you might tell him his choice of pronouns was incorrect. I am properly referred to as 'she' in English."

They watched until she walked out of the frame. Kirby sighed and did something on his phone and the video went blank. "Let's get me back to the car and decide what's next."

In the end they agreed what to do next was nothing. Given modern tools, the video could have been faked and they had no desire to become embroiled in the inevitable arguments and accusations. Alex finally summed up the experience. "At least, Kirby, you were right about there being 'something' out there. I hope it was worth what it cost."

"Definitely. And I'm going to pay for your Ph.D. to prove it. Then we'll go to Asia and check out the Yeti."

Author Intro

NANCY FOWLER

I am a California transplant, who has lived on the Olympic Peninsula (Port Townsend) for the last fourteen years. I enjoy exploring the natural beauty that surrounds us, and also reading, writing, gardening and time with friends. After a career writing detailed, logical reports on public policy, I developed an awareness that metaphor, abbreviation, and non-linear writing, tossed in with surprising use of language, presented a mental challenge to fend off advancing years. I write to acknowledge the specific realities and the existence of every individual, of every piece of this universe. My writing can be found in several publications, including various editions of *Tidepools, Porter Gulch Review, Songs of the San Joaquin, Poetry Bridge* and others. The last two years my poems have been selected by *Ars Poetica* at the Poulsbohemian. A collection of poetry is available at Writer's Workshoppe in Port Townsend.

Nancy can be reached at nmfowler@msn.com.

LET HIM MEET CROW

Each morning by nine, or maybe ten past,
the earnest poet hunches over a Formica table
near the window wall of the bakery café.
He slowly sips his mocha latte,
grizzled beard be damned. Tiny clouds of froth
drop now and then, on the poems-in-process
spread before him. He awaits the needed metaphor.

A steady tap-tapping, low on the glass near his booted foot,
demands attention, its persistence like an infant's cry
from the silent labyrinth before dawn.
He doesn't need to look to know it is the crow,
his every morning friend. But look he does, and waves,
a slight gesture, acknowledgement of presence.

Leveraging himself against the back of his slatted wood chair
and the table's wobbly edge, he slowly stands,
crumbled pastry in hand, then moves through the open door,
to feed the craving crow.

HIDDEN IN CLOSED DRAWERS

The insistence of rain drums on the roof,
taps on the nearby paned window.
I slide into dreams of that Kalaloch day,
when we slipped and skid into laughter,
down the wet bluff pathway,
to come upon a top-snail shell.
Its chipped brown- striped whorls revealed
an underlayment, pearly blue like the sky
swept free of storms.

If that shell had been left where it lay
among the tussled drifts of beach grass,
its sand would not have coursed, grain by grain,
from its twisted caverns into my tangle
of worn woolen socks, in brown and red and green,
to touch me again, as today I reach deep
into the open drawer, to ready for an ordinary day.

I walk our dog in the rain
alone.

TO CROSS THE COLUMBIA BAR

Along the coast of storms at the river of storms,
a cape, a disappointment of rock, mist-softened,
beckons the frigate close, and hides its fatal embrace
in the waves, with the tides pushing back against the current.

Lost in a tumult of unheard prayers,
the frigate's fate is sealed by the relentless rising
and sliding faces of breakers, crashing,
a glittering foam. It is finished so soon,
the breaking of this ship of the main,
flotsam scattered into the vagaries of conflicting currents,
drifting across and down ocean pathways,
to seemingly random destinations,
unfound by those who seek her end.

A barnacle encrusted board
with a remnant of the lost ship's name
drifts, drifts, drifts into sands
sifted through time, into the sea of trampled grass
secure above the tide line.

Author Intro

BONNIE DICKMANN

My husband and I moved to Sequim less than a year ago. We had vacationed here several times and fell in love with the nature we discovered. Rain forests and salt water are not a part of life in Wisconsin where we had lived our whole lives. We felt it was time to try new adventures.

My story idea came from a day when I was recovering from knee surgery at our home in Wisconsin on the shores of Lake Michigan. I spent several hours watching a lone goose on the beach and was thrilled to see it reunite with another flock.

I've always enjoyed writing and kept a journal for well over forty years. Writing is my way to celebrate life as well as help me through hard times. I was thrilled with the amazing writing community in Sequim and very happy to become a part of it.

Nature writing is what I love and while living in Wisconsin, the Department of Natural Resources printed several of my non-fiction pieces as well as my poetry. I've also had fiction published in the *Stoneboat Literary Journal*, the *Wisconsin Creative Literary Journal* and the Spontaneous Writing publication.

Spontaneous Writing by Twenty Courageous Writers is available on Amazon.com or from wideawakepublishing.com. Bonnie can be reached at bdwriter1223@gmail.com

GREY GOOSE DAY

I searched out the familiar warmth of my husband's back. Gently spooning him, I nuzzled close and kissed his neck. He rolled over and . . . damn, I wake up.

It's the same dream I had last night and the night before. I always wake up as he's about to kiss me. So, instead of wrapping my darling husband in a good morning embrace, I press the call button for the nurse to come in and help me get out of bed and into my wheelchair.

I remember when cuddling my husband wasn't just a dream. For the fifteen years we were married, I'd kiss his ear to bring him to the new day and he'd whisper, "Good morning, I love you." A mushy way to start the day, sure, but we were both old enough to appreciate the great relationship we shared, a relationship born from so much more than good sex. After our morning kiss, he'd rise, grab his robe, and amble downstairs to prepare coffee and let the dog out, giving me an extra five minutes to stretch out and savor the sensual feel of five hundred count Egyptian cotton sheets on my semi-naked self.

These morning habits were just one of many ways my dear Joseph spoiled me. We'd drink coffee staring out over the Strait of Juan de Fuca from our bedroom. Watching the antics of seagulls, ducks and geese became a quiet ritual to ease us into our long, busy days at work.

I met Joseph at a time when I'd given up on the idea of mating for life. It might work for Canada geese and grey wolves, but I didn't think I would ever find someone who would share my obsession with nature. I spent most of my free time hiking and bird watching. As a single at thirty-seven, I had learned to content myself with a great job in software sales and doing what I loved in my free time. I earned enough money to support my passion for glorious vacations in faraway places, searching out the indigenous feathered and furred creatures.

I met Joseph on one of these vacations. We were singles on a small boat cruise in Costa Rica. The brochure promised an intimate trip with a maximum of fifty passengers. You could take walks through the rainforest, scouting out colorful birds and exotic flowers. Or, just kick back and relax on black sand beaches. I didn't have to think twice about signing up. Out-going and athletic, I could pass for attractive with nothing more than mascara, so going on such a vacation by myself never bothered me. It was easy to pair up with other singles on these trips. Some of these trysts lasted a bit after the vacation, but usually, one of us would tire of emailing or long-distance phone conversations and drift back to our solitary ways.

But Costa Rica was different. Joseph and I both felt it shortly after we met. One evening, over a late-night martini, he shared the story of his first wife's unexpected death from a brain aneurism. He told me how the fear of ever repeating that pain had paralyzed his emotions and that, in the ten years since her death he hadn't found the courage to love again. But leaning against the ship's railing, feeling the gentle rock of the ocean beneath us, we both knew that was about to change. When he drew me into his arms, it felt like a long-awaited gift. I knew at that moment I just might have been given the opportunity to find my mate for life.

After the trip, Joseph and I decided to keep in touch. For two weeks after leaving our verdant Costa Rican paradise, we shared daily phone calls. Then came his invitation to visit him in Washington State for a weekend. I found a flight from my home in San Francisco to Seattle and booked it. I couldn't wait to see his home near the Dungeness Spit on the Strait of Juan de Fuca. Joseph had purchased it several years after his first wife's death when he realized that in order to heal, he would have to leave the past behind.

The first time I walked into his living room, the floor-to-ceiling windows facing the water drew me in with a sea siren's song. You could understand why words like "blue" just didn't do the color of the water justice. The cool rays of the March sun glinted off the water, turning it azure, cobalt and sapphire. Every shade of nature's watery palette was represented in the ocean's calm surface. As if on cue, two sea otters started playing on the stony bank outside his window. A Hallmark moment? You bet, but I was home and knew it. Little by little over our six-month courtship, I would bring my favorite books to his empty bookshelves, then some clothes to his closet. The final step came when I drove up to his home for a week's vacation and brought my cat, Simon to introduce him to Joseph's bullmastiff, Bogie. When our four-legged companions curled up together at our feet in front of the fire, we knew the deal was sealed. Joseph pulled a diamond ring from his pocket and proclaimed if our pets could live happily ever after, we should too.

After the wedding, I joined Joseph in his investment firm. We worked long and hard to build the company into a multi-million-dollar operation. We never had children. I guess both of us knew we were past the age of easy procreation. We loved working together, living together and vacationing together. We were happy and successful. Who needed anything more?

But success and money did nothing to protect us from tragedy. In our area of Washington, black ice occurs at least once most winters. It seals the roads with an invisible and unforgiving thin coating of ice, especially on the overpasses and bridges.

Joseph and I were coming home from a long day at work, and as we argued over some stupid small point of how to make our company even more profitable than it already was, he lost control of his BMW and skidded off the road. My last words to the man I'd waited so long for were, "Why the hell do you always think you're right?"

We flew off the overpass and landed on the roadway below in a terrible tangle of metal and flames. They told me Joseph died immediately. He was the lucky one. Now I get to start each day alone in our beautiful bedroom, waiting for a nurse to answer my buzzer.

It's Monday, so Maryann is on call. "Hello, Mrs. Davis. Lovely morning, isn't it?" Her bright greeting followed the soft knock at my bedroom door.

Does she have to sound quite that cheerful? Like a damn bunch of robins, chirp, chirp! "Yes, Maryann, I'm sure for some it is. What's on the agenda today?" I sneered as I struggled to raise myself up in the bed.

"You have an appointment with Dr. Foster at ten. We'd better get a move on and get you ready."

"That's right, I'd forgotten." I really felt no urge to keep track of my appointments anymore. I lost my cell phone in the accident and never bothered to replace it. Other people kept track of things for me now. Rich helpless invalids, with good health insurance, are lucky that way.

Maryann dropped the side of the bed and helped me sit up and slide into my wheelchair. That damn hospital bed didn't fit into the decorator's vision for the master bedroom, the room Joseph and I worked so hard to make our sanctuary.

Maryann helped with all my personal needs. I never could get used to someone putting me on and off the toilet, as well as being dressed in some less than couture outfit. No more designer heels and dresses. Now it was sensible shoes for my useless feet. No more fashionable suits, just slacks and blouses. I ate breakfast in front of the windows in the dining room with Simon and Bogie my only company. The silence was numbing. I stared out at the endless ocean of water, not really caring about the view. Sipping a tepid cup of coffee, I noticed a lone goose on the beach. I stretched up in my chair and scanned the landscape from east to west. Yes, indeed, the goose was alone. Joseph always said there was nothing sadder than a lone goose. You always see them in pairs or with a large flock.

"Time to go, Mrs. Davis." Maryann's voice pierced the fog of my melancholy thoughts. "We don't want to be late."

"Yes, let's get out of here," I replied, grateful to think of other things.

"Can you manage the seat belt, Mrs. Davis?" Maryann asked as she helped settle me in the car.

"Of course I can. It's my legs that don't work," I clicked the belt into place with just a bit too much force.

"I'm sorry, I just . . . "

"I know, never mind." I was sick of everyone waiting on me but, as Maryann reminded me daily, that is why I pay her. I'd always been fiercely independent. Joseph said that was what first attracted him to me. Thank God he wasn't able to see me now. I settled into my seat. We were off for our 'adventure' of the day, a trip to visit Dr. Foster.

After a cursory examination, the doctor came around his desk and sat in the chair next to mine. "Susan, we've done every test. It's been nine months since your accident, and there's nothing we've missed. Your inability to walk has nothing to do with your injuries from the accident. I'm sure of that. It's hysterical paralysis. We've talked about this before. You're living with the misguided notion that you could have saved Joseph, or that the accident was somehow your fault. None of that is true. Your paralysis is real to you and only you can heal yourself. I have a list here of some really good therapists. I'm sure that if you talk this out with someone," Dr. Foster paused and started writing something. "We can start therapy and . . . "

"Thank you, Dr. Foster. I'll be going now." I didn't need any damn shrink to tell me how guilty I felt. I spent every day knowing that my last words to the man I thought I'd never find, my mate for life, had been spat out in anger.

"Susan, please forgive me for being so blunt, but there's nothing else we can do. It's up to you now to reach out."

"Well, fine then. Goodbye." I turned my chair for the door and struggled to reach the knob.

The doctor came over and opened the door for me. "Here." He handed me a slip of paper. "It's my private number. When you're ready to get out of that chair, call me. I can line up all the help you'll need. I snatched the paper from his hand and let it drop into my lap, then hit the lever on my chair and sped down the hall.

On the trip home, I thought about that goose on the beach, how it just stood there, almost not knowing what to do or where to go. That's just how I felt.

We drove into the garage, and Maryann switched off the ignition. She turned to me and laid her hand on mine. "Mrs. Davis, I know it's none of my business, but I know a really great support group. It's a group . . . "

"A bunch of wheelchair women, no thanks." I started unbuckling my seat belt. "Just get me in the house. The last thing I need to do is hang out with a bunch of helpless women."

"It's not handicapped women. These women all lost their husbands very suddenly. You might find you have a lot in common with them."

"Yeah . . . thanks. Just get me in the house, okay?"

"Yes, ma'am. But really, sometimes being around others who have gone through the same things helps. They can understand your feelings in a way no one else can. I'll leave the phone number on your night stand."

"Thanks, that would be fine."

Maryann helped me into the house and got me settled in the bedroom. I wheeled myself to the patio doors and looked out over the Strait. It was one of those horrible November days when the grey of the sky and the grey of the water made it almost impossible to discern the horizon. A perfect day to sit and feel sorry for myself and that's what I wanted to do. So many thoughts swam through my head.

Hysterical paralysis, huh? In my previous life, no one would ever have called me hysterical. I used to be considered a competent career woman — smart and savvy with a temper to match. What happened that day of the accident to change all that? What happened to the woman I used to be?

Those last damn words to the man I loved were nasty and questioned my belief in his abilities. I'd always been the one to speak out in anger and apologize later. Joseph understood that and he would laugh at my Irish temper. He enjoyed sparring with me. Those ugly words were nothing more than me being snappish at the end of the day, but they were the last things he heard in this world.

Did he know how sorry I was? Did he know those words changed everything — forever?

As I sat in front of the patio doors, Simon jumped up on my lap and settled in. I absently stroked his fur and glanced out at the beach. It was empty. No humans, no otters, no birds . . . bleak, grey and quiet. Movement to the south caught my attention. I grabbed the pair of binoculars kept handy by the doors and set my sights on a dark patch. There, still on the beach, stood my lone goose. It just stood there. The melancholy of the grey day coupled with this solitary bird held me captive. Adult geese aren't supposed to be alone. They mate for life.

In spring, you see them in pairs, looking for a place to nest. By summer, their babies are ready to follow them around in the water and on long flights to anywhere. So when you see a lone goose, it's not a good thing. It usually means it has lost its partner to death. A lone goose will make any nature-lover mourn. It was the last thing I needed to see today. I pushed Simon off my lap and wheeled my chair back over to the fireplace to pick up a book. I couldn't think lonely or sad thoughts right now. What the hell? Even Mother Nature was in on the conspiracy against me.

The knock at my door brought a welcome interruption. "Mrs. Davis, I'm leaving now. Your night nurse is here. Just hit the button when you're ready for supper. I'll see you in the morning."

"Okay, thanks and, Maryann . . . sorry I was so crabby today. Just a bad day."

"No problem, Mrs. Davis. I put the phone number on the nightstand for you, think about it, okay? See you tomorrow."

She left and the quiet felt suffocating. I rolled my chair back to the patio door and looked for my avian friend. More than ninety minutes had passed and the lone goose still stood there, but now nearer to the house. It was clearly visible with the naked eye. It stood staring at the water and didn't move except to preen its feathers occasionally. Somehow I could not bear to leave my feathered visitor. Should I get Janet to go out here? Try to feed it? All these ridiculous ideas of trying to help this solitary goose, when my nature background knew I could do nothing to assuage its pain, whatever that might be. It needed to find a flock and re-join the world.

As I continued my vigil with the goose, a raucous group of seagulls came to the area where it stood. The gulls reminded me of all my well-meaning friends. They had descended upon me after the accident, bringing meals and flowers and sappy cards when all I wanted was to be alone with my grief . . . just like that goose.

Scanning the waters to the west, I spotted a flock of geese, maybe ten, floating peacefully out on the water, about a hundred yards off shore. I looked back at my lone goose, willing it to step into the water and swim to meet this flock, but it stood there, not moving. The flock kept swimming until they were straight out from my beached friend.

Come on. Come get the loner.

As if they read my thoughts, the flock turned from their easterly course and headed toward shore. That navigational change was just what my lone goose seemed to be waiting for. It waded into the water and swam out to meet the flock. After it caught up to them, they all turned and started swimming out again until I lost sight of them.

A small smile spread across my face. I turned my chair and rolled toward the nightstand. Sometimes it's Mother Nature that shows you the way.

Author Intro

LEONARD KNAPP

I am retired, but am neither as young as I was nor as old as I am.

My background has been rather eclectic. Born in Nebraska, I moved to San Diego, California as a senior in high school and attended San Diego State University, first as a music major and later on as an English major in the Education Department. After four years in the Air Force, where I was able to travel while stationed in Europe, I eventually accepted a position as an elementary teacher at the ripe old age of thirty.

Prior to teaching I worked in many areas: sales, human resource manager, ten years as a professional member of the Piano Technician's Guild — after studying and then becoming an apprentice technician — and I ultimately taught for about fifteen years and was a principal and administrator for about fifteen years.

After retiring in 2006, I moved to Sequim, WA and took up several hobbies, primary among them are weaving, knitting, and more recently, learning how to spin wool into yarn using both drop spindle and spinning wheel. Recently returning to a love of the written word, I can add writing, both poetry and prose, to my list of active pleasures.

Leonard can be reached at leonardknapp@mac.com.

THE WEDDING

A door closes behind her, ahead stretches a narrow carpeted aisle and a short walk to an uncertain end. She looks down the well-lit path into shadows. Before her, it leads to a sudden stop, pause, kneel and "I do." Do I? I will, won't I?

An oil painted crucifixion scene fills the alcove at the end: mute witness to her action or portent of the future? Whether it approves or disapproves she can't tell, but its presence makes her somehow less comfortable. Not panic, just a vague feeling of unrest as she contemplates the rows of expectant faces turned toward her, waiting, watching.

Music from a concealed organ swells urging her forward, the steady beat insistent, almost dragging her feet toward the waiting trio at the end of the aisle; only a dozen paces, but they stretch into infinity, into the unknown beyond. Is this it, is this her future, the closing off of options, enclosing her in this narrow boxed in space? She feels a tiny frisson of fear as she takes her first step.

She begins. The thoughts behind her eyes concealed by the white veil. Her dress, made by her own hand, with its secret expansion panel, moves forward almost of its own volition.

HOW LEGENDS ARE MADE

Legends, even local ones, must have a beginning; some event, however mundane, that takes on a life of its own — grows legs and moves from event into the greater world as a living breathing tale — sometimes taking on legendary proportions through the telling and retelling.

One summer afternoon when I was a boy of twelve, I was witness to just such an event. It would be years before I recognized the legendary potential of a single event; yet I believe I felt a tingle of its potential even then.

It was a hot day, late in the afternoon, humid with giant cumulus clouds mounding high in the air. Birds were chirping, insects were humming, and sweat tickled down my chest. A normal lazy day on a small farm in rural Nebraska. A green wall of corn stalks edged the yard and I stood on one foot listening to my grandfather and Mr. Childers, his friend who had just stopped by. They were talking about the usual topics: weather, crop prices, farm policies.

I paid only nominal attention to their conversation but watched my grandfather, his shirt sleeves rolled above his elbows and his overalls grease-stained as he lubed the tractor.

As they made small talk a bumble bee, hairy, black and yellow, buzzed loud and soft as it moved in an erratic fashion from petal to petal and flower to flower. The incessant buzzing began to intrude on my grandfather's concentration, and he stopped work and stepped into the shadowed opening of the machine shed. He reached into a cabinet just inside and took out a worn 22 rifle. Returning, he took aim, the barrel of the rifle making small adjustments as he tracked the insect.

Bang! Silence. The buzzing stopped, the bee vanished, and a look of amazement grew on Mr. Childers face as he let out a bellow of surprise.

"My gosh, Ray. I had no idea you could shoot like that," he said. He pounded my grandfather on the back in excitement. "That's the greatest shot I ever saw. You shot that bee right out of the air."

"It was a big bumble bee, not a honey bee," said my Grandfather.

"Sure, but you shot a moving bee out of the air with a 22 rifle. One shot and it just disappeared. Incredible!" he said.

I still stood to one side, out of the way, as Mr. Childers enthused over the amazing shot.

My grandfather returned to his work on the tractor. I could see Mr. Childers still shaking his head in awe as his pickup turned out of the driveway.

The birds began chirping again, bees still buzzed among the flowers, and the shadows lengthened.

I broke my silence then. "Grandpa, do you think Mr. Childers knew you had birdshot in the rifle?"

"Probably not."

"Should we tell him?"

My grandfather looked up, smiled, gave me a wink and continued his work.

My smile grew wide and nothing more needed to be said as we shared this tiny secret.

TOUCH

The tingling touch of skin on skin,
Whispering fingers, speaking slow

To bodies lulled with loving's glow.
All of these I've known and know—

But loneliness comes creeping, too,
When smooth-laid sheets stare mockingly

From empty rooms. And loveless nights …
But pauses in the flow of life.

BICYCLING

I pedal past the pedal-pushers,
Wheels a-whirling in the dust.

Thoughts of distant journeys taken
Quicken now, to thoughts of lust.

CHILL WIND

A chill wind
Stutters through the leaves,

Whining through bare wires,
It sings,
            And then expires.

IN MEMORIUM

The shadow of one's passing
Leaves a tear in the web of our lives,

Which, though it will be filled in time,
Changes the fabric's weave,

Altering its shape and design.
Just so, the passing of friends or family

Affect us in a permanent way.
And we are changed;

For their pattern's now
A part of us,

Forever.

THE SKY SHIP

Clouds flowed
Across the sky,
And as I stood in awe,

A mass of white
Took form and shape
And suddenly I saw

A mighty sky-ship
Sail along,
Spinnakers unfurled.

Through blue and empty
Heavens, trailing
Wisps of other worlds.

Proud prow plunging
Effortlessly,
As specters of long dead

Seamen mouth
Their soundless words,
"Come about!" they said.

A broken line
Of reefs was seen,
By lookouts up on high,

Then white-capped waves
Came lashing up
From jagged edges nigh.

"Come about!"
I saw them shout,
Though nothing had I heard.

I saw the sky-ship
Sail straight through
The reef and on, and on.

Masts blow away,
It dissipates,
And suddenly . . . it's gone.

CURRENTS

I feel them
move against my cheek –
my hair,
      my eyes.

Gently, gently,
      little, less,

and then,

away
      and gone.

WEATHERED LANDSCAPE

In looking at the weathered landscape ...

I see
   Deep ravines, ravaged by time,
     Brush, hoary with age,
      Empty spaces wind-swept and worn.

A once pristine nature, now scarred
   Shows mans' abuse.

Each misstep has left its mark.
A lifetime's cares in each crevasse.

What a devastating tool's the mirror
In the morning of life's waning.

Author Intro

MIKE MEDLER

I write because nature wills me to do it. I recently left a dystopian suburb of Seattle and retreated to the kneehills of the Olympic mountains, cut the cable, bought whiskey. Now I find inspiration from deep woods, less so from demons. Though they are there. You can find my words online at *Dodging the Rain, Nine Muses Poetry, Whispers, Plum Tree Tavern* and other poetry zines.

Michael's recent collection *Boundary Points* is available on Amazon.com.

DUNGENESS WOOD

Trees speak
soft soliloquy
bassoon tones;
this wood echoes
from crusted trunk
to basking canopy.
Words louder
than Dungeness
River as it rushes
long downhill
into the Strait
after a deluge.

Branches rub like
firm handshakes,
a rehearsal before
paradise calls. A
mourning, a dirge
for one fallen.

Roots thrust up
without grace,
a sad carcass,
food for fungi. I
look to the light,
fuel my stove
with long-gone
souls who once
sang without
dance, traded
tomes – poets
all. I am here,
Coroner of the
wood, to take
them down.

JOURNEY OF TREES

My journey takes me deep into pristine wood,
shadows, where fir trees sway, range sovereign;

echoes of song wrought of wind from distant sea.
Forms of boughs touch impaired thought,

phantom limbs shelter fitful dreams where
I sleep shrouded in that sweet pungent scent

that paints a colour of night fog ever creeping
through open bramble. I grow each breath

rooted in this ground. My knuckles will bleed
to protect it. But, seasons change, larger

than me. The avarice of others bends the wood
to their wills and this deep forest grows slowly

thinner; a spare moment, an acre of shattered
branch, bough and root wrought of greed.

PENN COVE OVERNIGHT

A single seabird call, distant in echoes, slices a leading edge
of night, begs dreams at anchor, like light fog moving

in from nowhere. This gray calm settles about, pervasive
sways, like the womb, like the warm belly of the boat

and any cold dreams are kept warm. An icy sliver of dark
passes in quiet whisper and a last illusion falls to water;

even ripples are the hollow echoes of a blue morning at anchor
on Penn Cove. Silver water, flat as canvas painted a rose-quiet

fury in pristine accord with eastern clouds, rises to welcome
this new mountain sun. For now, dreams and echoes are all

washed down with hot coffee and tobacco as the Cove yawns
and stretches; distant horns, closer motors turn. Dreams

remain as hovering mist; Penn Cove is now awake and all the sheets,
like pallid ghosts wet with morning dew, rise to greet it.

OPEN WATER

Beyond this mesh of brick,

beneath a sky of stone
where elusive shadows spill
from broken hedgerows,
I find my spirit lost
to a chasm of quiet fields.

A yearning for open water
and early dawns where
a bright confluence of mists
guides my thoughts, steers
me into pristine clarity,

Beyond this mesh of brick.

NAMING HER

Wandering, where my feet first touch
loose gravel bordering the river below,
pregnant with rain, with morning,
expectant of tastes. Air, heaviest

with mystery of cloudburst glistening
into daylight, I paused. Swallowing sound
of water, drowning in reverie, knowing
Rosemary in its most exuberant scent

could not compete with the sweet fragrance
of river at first light as it draws up the rush
of memory. I still remember you, the scent
of you, warm and whole in the fullness

of female. I remember you carrying
our first girl and I wonder now, my feet
dug into the edge of the scent of moving
water, why we did not name her 'River.'

BECAUSE

distance has widened the way lakes
take rain take tears solitude sings

single harmonies where fields
bend down to weaves of wave my

laughter falls fails to amuse
because now it has come to that

because now even birds trade empty
song and all the lakes have gone dry

because when we speak this way
words become leaves as they listen

to the roar deep in a Conch spiral
tell us of a region where lakes are

only of tears and our breathless
time bends back in unending arch

RAIN

There is this certain sense of sanity
that falls with rain. Empty quietude
remains, undefined, uncolored solitude
drifts where patterns shift and sway.

Distance undefined beneath ample gray;
all things lean beneath a burden
of replenished green. Words fall,
fail and are lost to shattered puddles

defined in sheen and stone, shifting
dances under foot and drop. Each
stanza tapped out on rooftops,
in-deciphered lines from a weeping

gray teletype. To know rain, to delve
into its wavering words, to have passion
nourished, to have this rain become
your tears, is to really know.

SOMETIMES BIRDS

laugh out loud at me, music non-percussive
with such force as to alter my emoji.
Sometimes birds fight amongst themselves,
battles best won with beaks not bowling balls.

Sometimes birds aren't there and I only see black
flickers through bony fingers of winter branches.
Sometimes they circle, drifting in phantom
cloud, eyes earthward looking for late lunch.

Often, they follow the path, a tunnel in shadowed
wood, leads them down to the river below me.
Sometimes they fling themselves into my
window, become dazed carcasses adorning ferns.

Most often, they sing, delight the air with
Morse chirps, Robin song reporting the weather.
Sometimes, but not often, they sing praises
of beauty for this sad broken planet of mine.

Author Intro

LINDA B. MYERS

After a marketing career in Chicago, I traded in snow boots for rain boots and moved to the Pacific Northwest. I spend enough time ruminating in these ancient woods and along the beaches to pop out a darn good story every now and again.

I write a monthly humor column for the *Sequim Gazette*, have completed eight novels, love the activities in our regional writer community, and think historical societies are goldmines. My selections for this anthology include a short story that takes place during halibut days, a memory of a sea voyage with my sister, as well as an excerpt from the second mystery in my Bear Jacobs series, *Hard to Bear*. My aim is to scare you a little and make you laugh.

Linda's novels are available on Amazon.com in paperback and ebooks. You'll also find Heidi Hansen and Linda at many gift fairs and craft markets, selling Olympic Peninsula Authors anthologies and more books by local authors. You can reach her at myerslindab@gmail.com.

FLATTIE SEASON

The auditorium door opens with a disruptive click. The people inside turn to stare at four men who enter and sit in the back. They are young, all wearing designer jeans, expensive shoes and t-shirts with humorous sayings or logos. The rotund woman in the front bangs the lectern with her gavel, bringing the audience back to attention.

Josie is sitting in a middle row. She has seen the men before, at the marina where she keeps her husband's boat. She'll get around to selling it one day, but she still enjoys it during flattie season. Halibut, she overheard the four men call the flat bottom feeders when they were talking to the captain of a charter boat. That proves they're out-of-towners. Josie wonders why they're here at this senior citizens meeting.

The rotund woman says, "We have visitors this afternoon. They've come from Los Angeles to talk to us. Gentlemen?" She leaves the lectern and takes a seat designated for her in the front row.

One of the men walks to the lectern. "I direct television commercials. We've come to film one here, and we would like one of you ladies to star in it." He appears nervous as he twists a ring around his little finger. Josie thinks perhaps it is difficult for this young man to address a roomful of seniors.

"It's a commercial for a brand of seafood from the Pacific Northwest. We will film in the home of the woman we select. She must be a very good cook." Then the director asks for nominations.

After the crowd murmurs for a while, they nominate several. Josie is surprised to hear her own name. She doesn't think of herself as a good cook anymore, because she no longer has anyone to cook for. Her children are married and gone. She prepares something for a church dinner now and then, but mostly she cooks for herself alone in the huge old kitchen.

The nominated women gather in a corner of the auditorium after the meeting. One man takes their pictures as they smile self-consciously. Another writes down their names and addresses. Josie wonders if she's doing the right thing by giving her information to him.

The next day she tends her roses, deadheading and pruning, before she walks to the post office for stamps. She purchases coffee filters and flashlight batteries at Swain's General Store. She has forgotten about the men from Los Angeles until she returns home and there they are, sitting on her porch and standing on her lawn.

Josie invites them in, expecting them to sit, but instead they walk around squinting at walls and furniture. They are most interested in the kitchen, specifically the white enameled gas stove. They defer to her, speaking as though they expect her to be hard of hearing. The director says, "Only two women are still being considered. You are one of them. Have you done any public speaking? Local theatre?"

Josie replies but has the feeling the director doesn't care about her answers, just wants to hear her talk. Finally he says, "We'll be in touch."

For the first time, Josie realizes she could actually be seen all over the country. Millions of strangers will stare at her. She will become a public person, and the thought troubles her. In the evening she calls her children in Chicago and Atlanta.

Her daughter is excited for her. "It will be fun, Mom."

Her son is less enthused. "They'll bring in lights and cameras and tear up your house."

Josie wonders what her husband would have said.

IN THE WORDS OF

By bedtime, she decides to do it. So what if the house gets messed up? She feels complimented to be chosen. Maybe she has qualities she's never recognized in herself.

The next day is one of those sun-filled beauties that Josie considers her reward for putting up with Washington rain. The mountains and islands shine and seem to have moved closer somehow. The four men appear in the late afternoon, and they discuss the weather until it becomes awkward. The director finally says, "We chose the other woman for the commercial. But we appreciate all your time."

The men leave. Josie watches the car pull away. She sits on her porch until the sun begins to fade and the temperature drops. Then she goes inside, locks the door, and closes the windows. The days are beautiful, but the nights can produce a chill.

FLATULENCE AT SEA

My sister and I were several hundred nautical miles from New Zealand. The sea was furious that night, with swells of thirty feet and more. Our cruise ship bobbed as insecure as a toy boat in a child's bath. Wind slapped us broadside, sending wild lashings of rain and spray crashing against our balcony door.

I am by and large a deep sleeper, but when your narrow twin bed shifts to a forty-five degree angle, that is a hint all is not well. I awoke with a snort, aware that strangeness was afoot in our totally dark 176 sq. ft. cabin, which is about the size of the large popcorn bag at your local Bijou.

I heard shuffling.

"Was I snoring?" I called out to Sis. We had been alone when the lights went out. Surely she must be the source of that shuffling sound unless a towel animal had come to life in the terrible storm.

"No," she answered. "But the room is making rude noises so I'm moving the table."

Okay, I was still half asleep. Maybe I had misheard. "Huh?" I asked, requesting clarification.

Almost simultaneously, I heard the sound of air being expelled through a narrow aperture from a smaller space to a larger space. Only a balloon or a Guatemalan flute or a fart is capable of this drawn out whistling sound. The kind of fart that one is trying and failing to release quietly, behind one's back as it were.

"THAT WASN'T ME!" Sis pronounced in all caps to the pitch black. And I was absolutely sure that it wasn't. She is the type who would hold it in forever vs create a public mockery.

The funny thing is that she never assumed it was me, either. She hadn't awakened me by shouting, "Ye gods, that's the last fruit buffet for you." Instead she said, "I think it's the wind against the balcony door. I was trying to push the table against the glass to stop it from shaking."

To punctuate, the room let loose with a much juicier blast, resonant and full, with the lingering echo of an M-16 firing in multiple bursts.

I began to giggle.

Sis finally joined in. "It must be the old man of the sea," said she.

"Thar she blows!" said I.

"Psssfffftttsssst," said the room.

It was three in the morning, in the dark, each of us in a bed as wide as a pummel horse. We should have been terrified by the extreme roll, pitch and yaw. We should have been memorizing the route to our muster station. We should have recalled childhood swimming lessons taught those many decades ago.

Instead, we laughed until we cried while the wind, forced through the door seal, puffed and squealed and rat-a-tat-tatted until dawn's early light.

HARD TO BEAR
PROLOGUE

Pain.

As Solana Capella came to, she groaned, her head pounding like a drill press.

What happened to my head? Ouch, my arm. Where?

Her eyes fluttered open and slowly focused on the feral eyes of a swamp monster staring back. Pain was joined by its old friend, fear.

But wait. Not a swamp thing.

The hollow-cheeked face wasn't really green. It was smeared with camouflage muck. The stranger was pushed up against her and seemed to be spreading the same green and brown ooze on her face.

Panic.

She yelped and began biting and scratching at Camo Man's hands. She inhaled the breath she needed for a championship scream, but his enormous hand clamped down over her mouth and pinched her nose, shutting down the air passages. She fought, but he tightened the grip. "Sshhh," he hissed low as a whisper. "They're coming. You must be very still. Do you understand?"

They're coming? Oh, God.

Now she remembered. She tried to control her fear of this new captor. She did her best to nod and, failing at that, blinked her eyes rapidly. Maybe he'd take that as, "Yes, I understand." He may hurt her, but at least he wasn't one of them.

Any old port in the storm, right?

She felt a hysterical bubble of laughter behind the hand over her mouth as it eased up, letting air rush into her lungs. He glowered a warning at her, then slithered down prone, pressing hard against her. That shoved her backside up to a damp cold wall of earth. The kind with spiders and centipedes and worms. She shivered, pressing back against him in hopes of moving her ass off the wall.

Solana was afraid she would suffocate as her face squashed into his slender chest. But some deep instinct of a small cornered animal told her to be ever so quiet, to freeze in place. Playing dead, she took inventory. From the little she could see, pressed against him, it appeared they were in a shallow, low cave. Roots from a million plants laced through the dirt and clay, holding its walls in place. It smelled of mold and rotten vegetation, overcoming even the fetid odor of filthy clothes and man sweat crushed against her nose. She could hear the sound of rushing water, and through the mouth of the cave, she was aware of only deep grey light. It must be nearly dark.

The pain reasserted itself. They had not marked her body. The scrapes, bruises and sprained wrist were from her wild flight. The real ache was buried deep within, raw and torn, from the rape. She shuddered against this stranger who now held her fate in his control.

Fear had been her companion since she'd been taken. It rose and fell like swells on the ocean. Now it was ebbing, as she accepted that Camo Man was helping her hide from them. When she felt his muscles tense, hers followed in lock step. Then she heard the sounds he was hearing.

Movement in the underbrush above. More than one hunter. Footsteps overhead, coming to a halt. Shuffling feet. Men swearing.

Flashlight beams crisscrossed the grayness in front of the cavern's opening. Then she heard in a voice she knew, "It's too dark. We'll miss her again. She'll be easier to track in the morning. She's too scared to make smart choices. Killing this bitch will be more fun than most."

They left. It was still. A minute, five, maybe a year. Then the man next to her moved back just enough for her to see his face. "They call me Ghost," he said. "You knocked yourself out trying to run under a tree limb. I brought you here. But we have to move on."

She considered his ragged camo jacket as well as the face paint. "Are you a soldier?" she whispered.

"Was. Can you walk?"

She nodded, although she was unsure how far she could go. Her sandals were no more than shreds now, one sole flapping loose against the bottom of her foot. She'd run so far, so fast that vine maple whips and blackberry thorns had cut her feet and her legs. The cowboy shirt she'd stolen was so big it had caught on snags, and now shreds flapped like homemade fringe. Same with the basketball shorts. But she was a fighter, and she would not give up. Her sister's life depended on it.

Ghost turned and slid on his butt out of the cave. "Follow," he said and she did, mimicking his action. As she slid out and down, he caught her just as her feet entered the freezing water of a fast-moving creek. She gasped.

"We'll walk in the creek for a while. No tracks to follow. No detectable odors unless they bring dogs tomorrow." Ghost headed upstream.

Solana looked back at the cave but could not see the mouth. It was hidden in the dusk behind the grasses on the bank. Her instinct was to go back there and hide forever. But she told herself it would not be so hard to see in the daylight. She had to swallow her exhaustion and fear.

Her baggy shorts rode so low on her hips that they dragged in the water. Holding them up with one hand, she followed Ghost. He seemed to sense where he was as the darkness became absolute, the journey only lit in patches where pale blue moonlight soaked through the forest canopy. He grabbed her uninjured wrist to lead her, and in time the freezing water dulled the pain in her feet. It seemed like a thousand miles until he stopped and pointed up the bank.

"Look," he said. The massive root system of an ancient Sitka spruce looked like clutching fingers in the moonlight. The tree must have crashed to earth many decades before. Now other spruce were growing from the nurse log which was at least twelve feet across near the base. The massive old roots swept out into an impenetrable arch of tendrils that intertwined with boulders rising above the muddy bank.

Ghost left the creek and pulled her up the bank to the far side of the roots where they jammed against a casket-sized chunk of volcanic rock. "Kneel here and crawl forward."

She did as she was told. On her knees she could see that there was room for her to shimmy between two tangled roots. She crawled through and found herself in a hollowed out cavern inside the fallen tree.

Ghost followed her in. He reached for a flashlight tucked inside the entrance and turned it on. "This is one of my hidey holes," he said to her. "Nobody knows it. We're safe. For now."

Solana watched him open the padlock of a battered foot locker with a key that hung on the chain with his dog tags. He lifted the lid of the locker and handed the flashlight to her. "You can leave it on for a little bit."

While he removed fur pelts from the locker and spread them over the bottom of the cavern, Solana flashed the light around her. She could see the space was a circle with maybe an eight foot diameter. "How did you do this?" She asked. "It's awesome."

"Burned it. Like some tribes hollowed out trees to make canoes." Next he rummaged out several strips of jerky. "Venison," he said, handing some of the dark, smoky slices to her. "Eat then sleep. We'll leave at daylight."

Solana took two of the pelts and crawled under them. If he meant her any harm, there was little she could do about it. She tried to chew the tough meat, but she was so tired. Too tired. The last thing she remembered was Ghost pulling out a satellite phone and calling somebody named Vinny. They made plans to meet. Solana was asleep before she heard where or when.

If you enjoyed this excerpt from Hard to Bear, *you can find all Linda's novels in print and eBook on Amazon.com.*

Made in the USA
San Bernardino, CA
03 September 2018